THE GOOD TEACHER:
HOW TEACHERS JUDGE TEACHERS

The Good Teacher: How Teachers Judge Teachers

By Richard Stone

PHILOSOPHICAL LIBRARY
NEW YORK

15 East 40th St., New York, N.Y. 10016
Library of Congress Catalog Card No. 78-130844
SBN 8022-2040-1
Published by Philosophical Library, Inc.
Manufactured in United States of America

"But who must train my child?" "I have just told you, you should do it yourself." "I cannot." "You cannot! Then find a friend. I see no other course."

A tutor! What a noble soul! Indeed for the training of a man one must either be a father or more than a man.

JEAN JACQUES ROUSSEAU, *Emile*

FOREWORD

This book tells teachers, parents, and others what a good public school teacher is, as defined by those who know the subject best—the teachers, themselves. More specifically, it tells how the teachers in one elementary school judged teacher quality. In other words, it tells who is the teacher other teachers admire.

For the last two of the six years I worked in this school I made notes on everything these teachers said about teacher quality. Whenever a teacher mentioned this subject, I took out a three by five card and made a note. I also asked plenty of direct questions. I believe this is the first time anyone inside a public school has observed and asked teachers what they think on this important topic.

Some of their comments I found comical. Others I thought quite insightful. All I choose to respect. In fact, I ended up believing that teachers are the best judges in the world of other teachers. Especially the older ones. After years of observing each other and passing the human material from one to another, these often become amazingly good at judging each other's workmanship.

Now the question comes up: "How typical are the teachers in this book—how representative of other teachers throughout the nation?" I can't claim that they are "the typical public school faculty." Perhaps no one faculty could be typical of every other one in the country. Certainly some parts of the life mentioned in this book are untypical—the way some parts of life in any school would be. Still I am convinced that these teachers judge teacher quality the way many other teachers do. They are neither so much better nor so much worse than teachers in thousands of other schools.

This book began as a term paper in a course at the Harvard Graduate School of Education. To the teacher of that course, John Herzog, my debt is great. I am also grateful to Robert Dreeben of the Graduate School of Education at Harvard. Thanks are also due to Roy Edelfelt, Edsel Erickson, Kenneth J. Lenihan, Dwight MacDonald, Harry Nichols, and Leslie C. Waldo. None of these people, however, can be held responsible for anything I say here.

Finally, I would like to thank the teachers of Pleasant Avenue School for their courtesy, patience, and expertise in answering the thousands of questions I asked over the years. They are the true heroes of this story. More than one of them will always be my idea of a good teacher.

Characters in this book do not have counterparts in real life. To protect the guilty, I have changed all names and descriptions of persons and places. With the exception of this effort not to embarrass individuals, this book accurately tells how the teachers in one school described a good teacher.

THE GOOD TEACHER:

HOW TEACHERS JUDGE TEACHERS

1

Our story begins the day I first reported to Pleasant Avenue Elementary School in Pleasant Valley, California, a suburban community just outside Los Angeles. The first person I met there was Jack Lacy, the principal. Jack was then 27, with plenty of wavy hair and broad shoulders which suggested that at one time he may have been an athlete. He wore a black and white sports jacket and looked like some prominent member of a yachting club–which I was to learn later he was.

His office, with its thick rug, leather chairs, and drapes looked like it belonged to some bank officer. I had not realized that school administrators had such beautiful offices.

Jack's phone kept ringing and his secretary kept bringing papers in for him to sign (and he seemed never to know where to sign), yet he kept the conversation going. Finally, he said that, though it was the superintendent who had hired me, still he approved of me too. Then he took me down the hall and showed me the gymnasium.

Though I always liked Jack, still I must admit that among teachers he had a reputation as a blockhead of the first degree. He had a mind like a sieve. Everything you told him, he promptly forgot. As the saying goes, "In one ear, and out the other." Everything in life hit him as a complete surprise.

Naturally, this made for much conversation in the faculty lounge. "He'll agree with everything you say," said one woman. "Then he'll walk down the hall and forget all about it. Five minutes later he will deny he ever talked with you."

"I tried to explain the details of our bus trip to Los Angeles to him," said another. "He just sat there numb, like a dummy. He did not say a thing. So I asked another teacher to explain it to him. She did. He still just sat there, blankly. If you ask me, he's not any too bright. I'm thinking of leaving this school, by the way. I've just about made up my mind."

Jack had absolutely no interest in things academic. He never talked about the latest educational studies, about books, or even about the children. Some of the teachers said that years ago he had made a mistake in his choice of a vocation, but now he was too old to do anything about it, and accepted his lot. He spent most of the day reading one paperback novel after another. He did not even bother to put them away when people came to visit him. Indeed, one might get the impression that he was begging the superintendent to fire him. He seemed to want out.

The routine of running a school bored him stiff. Take, for example, the task of delivering stern, moralistic lectures to the little boys whom the teachers had sent to the office for punishment. This chore takes up a good part of the principal's day. Such talks are supposed to improve the deportment of the boys. They are expected to return to their classrooms vastly improved human beings.

However, Jack delivered his lectures in such an indifferent and hopeless manner that the children, instead of dreading trips to the principal's office, rather liked them. His standard approach went something like this. "Tommy, what is this your teacher tells me? She says you have been reading a bad book. What is the title of the book? Oh, you have it with you now. Here. Hand it to me *The Ninety-Seven Positions!!*

"So it's all the way down to the gutter, eh, Tommy? Next comes strong drink, then bank robbery, then the penitentiary, and finally the electric chair. Now you go back to class until I can think up some suitable punishment for you!" He always smiled pleasantly on dismissal.

"Next case!" he would shout to a long line that always stood outside his office door. Teachers were beginning to complain that their discipline cases, instead of returning reformed and chastised, came back relaxed and refreshed.

Of course, on days when he was away at some meeting at headquarters (and he was often at a meeting at headquarters), the office filled with bad little boys. To take part of the work burden off herself, the secretary fell into the habit of giving jobs to some of these. And on a more-or-less typical day you would see one running the mimeograph, another putting letters in the teacher's mail boxes, and a third stapling together the pages of one more purple pamphlet.

Many a teacher who had sent his worst discipline case to the office in the morning found to his amazement in the afternoon that this mean kid was actually running the place. For the secretary had a tendency to leave the office for innumerable coffee breaks. "You want to know who is answering the phone and running the office right now?" one teacher would ask another. "The dumbest kid in the school. Doing a rather good job too."

One wondered how a person like Jack with so little interest in the work could hold down such an important position. The answer is that, while Jack had his weaknesses, he had some strengths, too. He was, to begin with, a very charming person. He liked people. He wanted to be liked, and he was liked.

He was also fun to be near. He cracked jokes continually. Indeed, his whole personality seemed to say that a gay party was about to begin, and you were invited.

Jack had friends all over town–especially among community leaders. Indeed, when he finally came to work in the morning–at around 10:00–the first thing he did was pick up the phone and ask some friends how they had survived the party last night. Considering the number of hours he put in at such parties, perhaps he did not have such a short work day after all. Maybe it all added up to business.

Sometimes people outside the profession think of all educators as necessarily erudite, refined, and even faintly spiritual men, something above the ordinary. They imagine that these must spend their evenings reading from the works of Pestalozzi, Freud, and Dewey. Either that or writing articles for learned journals. Quite often, however, the men who do these things remain mere classroom teachers for life. They work for other men who know an even better subject–politics.

Well, maybe this is as it should be, for a public school is hopelessly dependent on the good will of the taxpayers. Its greatest need, therefore, is men who can charm people in carload lots.

Charm them, Jack did. He was a past master at that. Jack was particularly good at handling the ladies. No doubt because of his sensationally good looks, he was able to convince the plainest housewife who ever washed her husband's overalls that he had just fallen in love with her.

"Can you imagine," one of our men once asked, "what he must mean in the life of some of these local women? I mean, here is the husband, a street cleaner, who sits drunk in front of the television set every evening in his undershirt. Then one day she walks up to the school to see why her no-good son has been expelled again. And this handsome young principal plainly indicates that, if it were not for the ring he wore . . ."

I doubt, however, that Jack and his numerous girl friends ever did anything wrong. For Jack was in reality a fine, up-standing family man. Giving tired housewives the feeling that they still had the power to attract, giving them a glimpse into his glamorous world of cocktails for two, country club dances, and secret love affairs, was simply one of his administrative skills–and very nearly his only one. So, of course, he used it continually.

I suspect that these women were also a little too much awed by his title. Every day, it seemed, some mother came to the office to speak to the principal about the quality of education her child was receiving. No, she did not want to speak to any teacher. Only the man at the top would do.

I heard more than one teacher say, pointing to the office door, these women could not possibly be making a bigger mistake. Why, plenty of our teachers knew much more about education than our principal knew.

I don't know why this should have surprised me so much. Surely I must have heard of incompetent persons in high places before. Maybe I had always thought of education as above that sort of thing. Why, to me it was like the Church. I had never dreamed of incompetency *there*. Whatever the reason, Pleasant Avenue teachers taught me that in a public school title and rank serve as very indifferent indicators of a person's quality.

2

Next I met some of the teachers. I suppose a reasonably good example would be Bill Bartholomew. He stayed at the same rooming house I stayed at. Young–or at least seemingly young–Bill was also infinitely polite, refined, and very intelligent. He could not pass a book or magazine without pausing to read some of it.

Every evening he went to a meeting in some town near us. For Bill was an official in the county teachers' association. All this visiting around gave him a tremendous fund of knowledge about schools and teachers. He was particularly erudite on the subject of salary schedules.

Before he got married (Bill finally married one of the teachers' association officers he was continually visiting) he and I used to drive around, looking at the homes and schools in the towns near Pleasant Valley. In one community all the homes would be large, surrounded by trees, and set well back from the quiet streets. The cheapest cost around $35,000.

In other communities, such as ours, all of the little houses were set close together. There were no trees, no sidewalks, and no place for the children to play, except in the streets. Garbage cans sat on the front lawns because there were no alleys to put them in. In such a town, the most expensive house would cost around $15,000.

You might not believe it, this very intelligent young teacher used to say, but there was often a big difference between the quality of the teachers in the more wealthy communities and the quality of those in poorer ones. That, he said, was because the taxpayers in one town offered higher salaries, better working conditions, superior living accommodations or something else to attract them. The superintendents there received more applications than they could ever handle. From these, they picked only the very finest.

In other locations, however, the community had so little to offer that the officials there had a tough time getting any kind of teachers at all, good or bad. As one of our other young men expressed it, to keep these schools going, the administrators had to empty out the penitentiaries, the insane asylums, and even the graveyards. What he meant was they had to use the human material other school districts had either thrown out or long ago retired.

Let's look into this matter of salaries in a little more detail. While teachers theoretically are not supposed to be motivated by desire for personal gain, still money does attract some, as it does in all professions.

Districts around us that paid well received a fantastic number of applications. Beverly Hills High School, not too far away, for example, received in 1963 no less than 2000 applications, and that for no more than five or ten openings. Their pay scale that year went as high as $14,000 for plain classroom teachers, no specialists.

Districts that did not pay well, however, had a terrible time finding teachers. In 1963, when our pay scale was low in comparison with other districts, many of the classrooms had no professional teachers at all. As substitutes, the superintendent had to hire college graduates who had never taken an education course in their lives, and even housewives with just a year or two of college. I remember one old lady 71 years old, who could hardly walk, much less teach—and that was her first year of teaching.

In those days, I often heard our superintendent groan that better-paying districts were taking away the few good teachers we did have. "The minute we get a good teacher," he once said, "some well-paying district hears about him and steals him away from us."

Naturally, there was considerable agitation to raise salaries—in order to get teachers of any kind. Some school board members joined in. For they too believed that mere money attracts many a good teacher. How right they were. By the end of this study, after salaries had been raised considerably, our superintendent began to receive more applications than he could handle, and the teachers began to comment on the high quality of new teachers we were getting.

"Are you a pre-medical student?" I asked one particularly talented young man. I could not believe that anyone that intelligent would want to spend his life in a fifth grade classroom. "No," he replied. "I intend to make a career out of public school teaching." Good grief, I thought to myself. He's a better teacher than I am, and he just started yesterday morning.

Two of these young men received offers from colleges, but they turned them down. Grade school teaching, one said, paid so much that he would not dare leave. This man, a $9,600-a-year third grade teacher, received an offer of $4,800 from a nearby junior college. When he asked the advice of one of our administrators, the older man replied, "Do you realize what you would be in Los Angeles on $4,800? You'd be a bum, that's what."

Another attraction of a wealthy district is superior working conditions. To some teachers, these can be even more attractive than higher salaries. In wealthy districts around us, for example, a class of low I.Q. students would have only ten or twelve students in it. In other districts, however, such a class would have thirty or so. Such pupils are a terrible burden on teachers. Teachers of such classes, our teachers said, are always sick—from physical and nervous exhaustion. After one year with such a class many a fine young man or young lady leaves teaching permanently.

In fact, in a poor district any pupil at all is likely to be difficult to teach. Poorer districts, or even poorer neighborhoods, contain many a disruptive child. Our people objected to such children's manners, morals, and work habits. Such pupils often hate education. Any teacher must work extra hard to teach them anything at all.

I recall one kid who came to us from the slums. Though still in grade school, he made continual off-color remarks to the girls. These complained to their mothers, who of course, called his teacher. He also fought with the boys, fighting being something he was good at. To top it all off, he even used to razz his teacher. "Say," he used to say by way of entertaining the class, "you old men sure are hard to get along with."

Even if they are not disruptive, children from poor homes often have seen less, heard less, read less, and experienced less than more fortunate pupils. Their parents may not have had the time or energy to take them on trips or even to talk to them. If you mention the public library, they wonder where it is. They do not know the meaning of hundreds of ordinary words. Some have never been five miles out of town. No matter what their I.Q., such children require extra work.

In poor districts there is always an emergency. Either there is a shortage of texts, desks, paper, or something else. Sometimes this mean living brings out the meanness in people. For some teachers will fight over what little equipment there is. In wealthy districts, on the other hand, the administrators create much harmony by simply buying everything everyone wants. It is amazing how many problems you can solve with mere money.

Sometimes superintendents and principals in affluent districts–who naturally are in a position to be selective–have devoted lifetimes to picking and keeping the very finest of teachers. To work among such people can constitute a kind of post-graduate course. On such faculties work standards and expectations are so high that any new teacher soon finds himself acting up to his very best. He can't afford to slump. Incidentally, some of us need the company of such quality teachers to keep us good.

Other districts hire persons of such low quality that their best teacher is actually not as good as the worst teacher in some nearby rich district. This gets dramatically demonstrated when their superintendent gets fired—and promptly fails to get a position as a classroom teacher in some other district.

I once heard a teacher summarize the difference between the two types of districts this way. "One," he said, "develops you. The other just screws you." He might have been right. Few teachers are able to rise much above the level of the rest of the teachers in a school. Some may. But not many.

However, though the teachers I talked to and listened to said they believed that those who were picked to teach in wealthy districts are almost invariably good ones, still they had to admit that a few good ones remain in poor districts, too. For some teachers like to work where they grew up, or where their friends are. Indeed, the teachers in the poorest districts in Arkansas and Mississippi may not realize it, but every time this subject came up in our faculty lounge, someone was sure to remind us that some pretty good men and women choose to remain in such places, giving their lives to help.

Sometimes the reputation of the district for academic excellence—which is almost always synonymous with its wealth—provides the attraction. A few days before the opening of school one year, our superintendent looked out over a roomful of new teachers at an orientation meeting. "Well," he began pleasantly, "perhaps we should introduce ourselves. Let's start with this pretty little lady over here." He pointed to a very plain-looking person in the first row. "Just give your name, and where you used to teach. That will be enough. In that way, we will get to know you."

The old man was surely right, for when a teacher gives her address, she tells plenty about her quality. Thus, when one young lady mentioned Newton, Mass., the superintendent looked up suddenly. "Say," he exclaimed, "you must be good. That's an excellent system. They hire only the very best. Welcome."

Such quality districts are usually well-known inside the profession. But not so well-known outside. The average Pleasant Valley parent, for example, thought that since our district and all those in the surrounding area were licensed by the State Department of Education, then all must be of roughly equal quality. Why, there was a certificate from the State Department hanging in the hall of our schol, wasn't there? What further proof could you want?

Only our teachers were subtle enough to realize that there could be tremendous differences between the quality of the product dispensed in one district and another. So big, in fact, that the teaching in one district might be a whole year ahead of that in another. When a child moved from an excellent district to an inferior one, he might receive an automatic promotion, say from the fourth to the fifth grade. "That other district is one year ahead of us," some teacher would explain.

At the opposite extreme, there were other districts where the quality of education was pretty low. In one, for example, when a child stayed home sick all one year, they passed him anyway. On testing him, they found that he had learned just as much watching television all day, as he would have in one of their classrooms. Maybe they were right.

It is to these academically excellent districts, incidentally, that teachers often send their own children, knowing the score very well. Several of our people moved to a community miles from Pleasant Valley and went deeply in debt buying homes, so that their children might get the first-class education that could be obtained only there. Readers wondering about academic excellence of different districts might ask the question, "Where do the teachers send their children?" If the answer is "The next town," look out.

3

Over the years I heard teachers say that even within the same district there can be a difference between the quality of the teachers in one school and the quality of those in another. Each principal, attracts and keeps a certain quality of teacher–and repels others. For example, one school in our system was what members of the profession call a country club. That is, it was a school in which the principal takes it easy on the teachers, they adopt a lenient policy toward the pupils, and everyone tends to enjoy life.

Teachers there sat in the faculty lounge as long as they pleased. Their friends watched their classes. For they had adopted a popular new educational technique by which one teacher watches over two classes, while the second rests in the faculty lounge. No matter how much the superintendent and the assistant superintendent raved, the teachers all did as they pleased.

This inspired teachers in other schools to make jokes. "Why," one said, "a good teacher over there is one who sticks around for lunch." He was referring to the fact that a few teachers on split session did not wait until the appointed hour, 12:00, before going home. They went home at 11:00.

One day our principal asked if I would go to the Country Club school and work one day to help their new physical education teacher get started. But the next morning my car would not start. By the time I got there, 9:00, I was one hour late. I went immediately to the principal's office to explain my tardiness.

But I found the office door locked. A teacher who happened to be strolling down the hall explained that the principal, and many of the teachers, had not come to work yet. They always dragged in late. "The office never opens until around ten o'clock," he added. I was astonished. Even though by most people's standards I was an hour late for work, by their standards I was an hour early.

The teachers called another school in our system the Work House, and here again the reputation of the school was greatly influenced by personality of the principal. This man worked himself and his teachers extremely hard. If you were not a very energetic and otherwise high-quality person, you would not fit in there.

A third school in our system was called Academic Siberia. The principal there did not get along with his teachers. He had a mind not so much bright as it was tricky and crafty. For example, he held the opinion that to get more work out of teachers, you should encourage them to spy and complain about each other.

We heard stories of secret trials at which the accused was not allowed to testify. "Two teachers complained about the noise in your room," the principal of Academic Siberia would tell a teacher. But he never gave the names of the complainers. This caused every teacher to suspect every other. It also caused many teachers to develop a strong dislike for each other.

The turnover rate there shot sky high. One year it was fifty per cent. This when the national average was something like ten per cent.

Now, just as teachers flocked to get into some schools, such as ours, they tried like crazy to stay out of this one. Indeed, some principals kept control of their more obstreperous teachers by threatening to send them there. On account of the staggering turnover, the principal of Academic Siberia was always short of teachers–of any quality. And Academic Siberia did tend to fill up with some very undesirable characters.

I remember one time I was arguing with Jack. I don't remember about what. All of a sudden Jack said: "Suppose they need a good physical education teacher over at Academic Siberia some time–and we know they will. Somebody downtown might want to send you there. I might not be able to argue them out of it. Ever think of that?"

I was one well-behaved physical education teacher for a relatively long period after that.

So location also tells something about a teacher's quality, I said to myself. Well, here was one more way teachers judge teachers, and I made another note on a three by five card.

4

Another opinion of Pleasant Avenue teachers on the subject of teacher quality was this. They believed that the larger the community the more the attraction for teachers—thus providing city administrators with a wide choice, from which they could at least attempt to select only the best.

There was a cut-off point, of course. Our people did not consider work in mammoth cities, such as New York and Chicago particularly attractive. There, finding a decent place to live, non-English speaking students, race riots, and crime in the schools made life trying for the teachers. The most attractive locations to us were cities of 50,000 to 500,000, or wealthy suburbs just outside such cities.

A surprising number of teachers had begun their careers in small towns—then moved to cities or the suburbs just outside of cities. In fact, there seemed to be a definite trend for the typical Pleasant Avenue teacher, when he was just out of college, to spend one or two years in some small town. There he perfected his professional skills by practicing—and sometimes making some pretty bad mistakes—on the small town children. Then, as soon as he learned what he was doing, he immediately moved away—and was replaced by another well-meaning fumbler straight out of formal school.

But small town parents did not object. Indeed, they seemed to expect all teachers to move along. For they could afford to pay only beginner's salaries. If too many teachers were to stay, this might cause embarrassment all around.

And what caused this exodus? Well, superior living conditions and cultural advantages, for one thing. Intellectuals —even middle-brow ones—have long been drawn to cities. There they have a wide choice of housing and a selection of friends with similar tastes. There they also find the shops, restaurants, theatres, and libraries so dear to the hearts of members of the middle class.

Larger communities even contain more marriage prospects—an item of no small importance in the life of a young person. A young man once said that in the small town where he began his career there were exactly two women in his age bracket. One did not like him. And he did not like the other. So that took care of the social situation for that year. "You can't realize the number of pretty, young teachers in a small town who go through the whole year without a single date," he said. "Of course, there are plenty of married men who would be glad to date them."

Small town life can be trying for teachers in other ways too. Here social life is often composed of a few wealthy ranchers, a few bums hanging around the local saloons—and no middle class people at all. There are no people for the teachers—married or unmarried—to associate with. Ranchers and cattlemen's daughters, incidentally, date ranchers' and cattlemen's sons—not sheepherders or school teachers.

In many a small town, the center of culture may actually be a drugstore soda fountain with its accompanying magazine rack. Even if the teachers pile into their cars and drive to the next town, all they might find would be another drugstore soda fountain, plus a few cheap bars. These are usually inhabited mainly by old men who never get off the same bar stools. They seem to be glued there.

It is all very well to argue that the teachers out in Hopeless, Iowa, or Dismal Corners, Montana, may subscribe to *Encounter, The New Republic,* and the *New York Times.* But life has a way of not happening like that. Soon, the small-town teacher is reading nothing more stimulating than the local weekly newspaper and singing like mad in the church choir–simply because there is nothing else to do. Even locals warn new teachers: "Don't let this place get you down. Keep your chin up, boy."

Few people realize how little time the radio station in Godforsaken, Kansas, devotes to classical music. Maybe one symphony per week. And you are lucky if the local movie theater runs one decent picture per month.

Then there is the fact that in small towns the residents sometimes get to know each other a little too well. Teachers, being local celebrities, get watched especially closely. Every move they make is not only noticed but also interpreted. If your car (which everyone in town knows well) is parked outside a bar, then every passer-by knows where you spent the evening. If you go to the movie alone some night, the lady at the ticket window wants to know if you tried to get a date but got turned down. Every businessman knows exactly how much you make–and, therefore, how much respect you are entitled to.

Sometimes, teachers get to know townspeople a little too well too. Oh, the unkind stories that we told of life back in Possum Trot, or Tree Squeak, or some other lovely but dying little community. One teacher told of a mother who sat drunk all night in a bar, then came out to find her children frozen to death in the car outside. Another told of a rancher who sold the whole spread to the son on his 18th birthday for $1, so he could go on relief. We had any number of spicy stories of mothers forever in bed with the telephone lineman–or the grocery delivery boy. No teacher ever wanted to go back–even for a visit.

Small town politics can also be murder on teachers. Contrary to popular belief that all small towners are just one big, slap-happy family, these towns are often full of strife. The local teacher always ends up in some war or other. He has to. If he is a Catholic, then he automatically belongs in one camp. If he is a Republican, then he automatically gets certain other people for enemies. Larger cities, on the other hand, confer on the teacher the blessed gift of anonymity—which can be very restful and peaceful.

Consider the low work standards in many a small and impoverished district. When I reported to my first coaching assignment in a rural district, I was amazed to see another man standing in the gym blowing a whistle. The dear old superintendent had carelessly hired two men for the same position. This superintendent then asked if I would mind teaching French. I replied that I did not know anything about the subject. "That doesn't make any difference," he said. "The kids don't either."

Two of our teachers told of districts where the members of the Board of Education would never allow a Catholic to stay on the staff. They hired one every year to serve as vulgar window dressing. But they would never allow one to last more than two years. Other small towns would not hire Jews. Maybe all this has since changed. Maybe not.

At this point I can hear the groans of anguish of some readers. What about the local merchant's wife who devoted nearly an entire lifetime to the community—because the teacher shortage after World War II never ended? What about the rancher's divorced daughter who returned from New York and buried herself in school work? They could have taught in any system in the country. Did they pack their bags and head for the city every time they heard that the teachers there just received a $300 raise?

What about the outdoors types? A few good teachers want to stay where the best hunting and fishing are.

Obviously, small towns hang onto many a good teacher. Still, as the great exodus out of all small towns continues, it takes with it much tax revenue. Unless the school district is parked over an ocean of oil, then, as the district wealth declines, the schools may decline too. Those teachers who choose to remain behind may, therefore, find it increasingly difficult to answer one question. Why?

5

No doubt you have heard the expression town and gown. This refers to animosity sometimes found between people outside the school and those inside. Since the middle ages, townspeople and teachers have battled for one reason or another. The absence or presence of this ill-will has an effect on the attractiveness of a community to schoolteachers.

Some districts have a long history of good feeling between these two groups. Long before the salary committee can present its demands to the school board, the board announces a handsome raise. In fact, there is no salary committee. For there is no reason for one. You hear that the only reason teachers leave such places is death or pregnancy. Such districts (not all of them wealthy, by the way) have never had a shortage of applicants.

Other districts have a long history of bitter combat. All one reads about these is that the taxpayers have turned down the budget again, or worse, that all the teachers have gone out on strike.

In some extreme cases, teacher associations, such as the National Education Association, the state education association, or some other teacher organization has warned its members, for God's sake, to stay out. Naturally, the local superintendent contradicts this, saying that, as a matter of fact, this district has never in its history received so many applications. However, it has been pointed out that teachers who rush to get into trouble-laden districts are often hard up for work. Some are uncertified. A few are sex perverts and other degenerates thrown out of other districts. These realize all too well that this superintendent is desperate for any kind of teachers at all.

This is also the kind of district that university professors warn their students to avoid. They explain that if you work in such a strife-riddled district, some of its reputation is sure to rub off on you. If you teach there, then you spend the rest of your life explaining that all the trouble people read about was caused by other teachers. Only you were pure. Oh, yeah!

Among teachers, the Pleasant Valley School District enjoyed rather a good reputation. Most Pleasant Valley people respected the school and the teachers. For example, even though it was just an average community, the taxpayers passed every budget and bond issue overwhelmingly. In fact, one year, when the Catholic priest warned all parishioners to turn down the budget, they passed it anyway.

Furthermore, it was for the most part, a friendly community. Everyone had just moved in from someplace else. There was no such thing as the parents being the establishment, and the teachers mere transients. Everyone was out to make friends. It was like the old West all over again, like the land of beginning again. If a teacher acted halfway decently, he could have all of the friends he desired.

When I stood in line at the supermarket checkout counter, parents ahead of me insisted that I move to the head of the line. When I broke my leg, the first time I walked outside on crutches, a car skidded to a stop on the highway. One of the mothers got out, left her car standing there blocking traffic, and rushed over to ask if there was any place she could take me.

Pleasant Valley children were also pretty nice. That same time, when I had foolishly broken my leg, I lay in my rooming house wondering how I would ever get my paycheck. Then I heard downstairs the sound of many little voices.

Some of the children had convinced their father to take

them to my rooming house. He explained that his children had been nagging him for days, saying that Mr. Stone always liked to get his mail promptly. And there it was stacking up in the school office. I talked this over with several teachers and they said that parents and children could make many a quality teacher want to stay on and on in what might strike the visitor as a not particularly glamorous community. Perhaps this explains why some of the best teachers in the world work in some of the poorest districts. In this sense at least, our teachers said that every district gets pretty nearly the teachers it deserves.

6

One teacher who joined us late one year but who quickly turned out to be everyone's idea of a good teacher, was Tom Fitzgerald. A big tough-looking ex-paratrooper in his late 20's, Tom went through life winning one scholarship after another. He taught third grade.

You would think that a man that intelligent would belong in high school or college teaching. Yet there he was, perfectly happy in a third grade classroom.

Tom illustrates another belief of the Pleasant Avenue teacher: what an elementary school needs is not more unintelligent and childlike types to get down to the children's level–in case there is such a thing. New methods of teaching, some very intelligent pupils (who required extra work), and some very intelligent colleagues too created a need for just as intelligent people in a grade school as in any other kind of school.

Our teachers often said that elementary education was no consolation prize for those unsuccessful at the high school level. All of us, it seemed, knew people who had failed at grade school teaching. A number of times the fifth and sixth graders were in danger of taking over the school and throwing the teachers into the street, grade school or no grade school.

Many Pleasant Valley residents believed that a high school teacher ranked one notch above an elementary one. In their minds, doctors came first, then lawyers, then local businessmen, then high school teachers, then elementary teachers, who ranked just a little above the clerks in stores—who in turn barely outranked the garbage collectors.

They thought a high school teacher handled more difficult and therefore more prestigeful material—Trigonometry, Chaucer, the Constitution of the United States. In fact, some saw the high school teacher as a close relative of the university professor.

However, locals saw a elementary school teacher as a close relative of the baby sitter. "Name the days of the week for me, Tommy," they knew a more-or-less typical elementary school teacher would say every day. "Now, think, Tom! Think!"

"Monday, Thursday, February, and March," some little boy would say, hitting his head occasionally to stimulate the sluggish mechanism inside.

"Dear God," the teacher would softly exclaim, raising saints' eyes to heaven. "And to think the big test begins next week, too! What am I to do with these youths?"

Every day, they knew, the typical Pleasant Avenue teacher had to march his class to the toilet and advise the little boys to try hitting that target—the way the Air Force bombardiers do. Then, after ten or twenty minutes, he had to shout in the doors of both the boys' and girls' toilets and order everyone to turn it off—through or not. Otherwise, some of the children would spend all day in the toilet—happily working the polished silver levers and handles there—and forgetting all about the classroom.

From this description you might think that we at the elementary level must have been eating our hearts out envying those "up" in the high school. Let me assure you that we did no such thing. All our people were absolutely sold on working with elementary kids. We loved it.

I loved working with children of this age. The little girls all want to marry you. You have to keep shoving your lap under your desk to prevent them from sitting on it.

"If you ever teach kids of this age," a Pleasant Avenue teacher once told me, "you'll love them so much you'll never want to teach any other. Three years in this business, and you're hooked for life." All I can say is it's true—every word of it.

As a matter of fact, many of us in the elementary grades said we did more teaching than they did 'up' in the high school. Many high school teachers have to spend much of their time working on discipline. This means less time for teaching.

"For Christ's sake," I once heard an auto shop teacher scream at his dull, lazy pupils, "stop goosing each other with that air hose! You want to blow out someone's bladder or appendix? I seen that happen once." What was so prestigeful about that kind of teaching?

Besides, we happened to know that not all high school students are eager young scholars, questing after the truths contained in the works of Archimedes, Shakespeare, and Jefferson. Some hit dope. Others carry knives. A few have prison records.

All too often the cute grade school kid who hangs around his teacher's desk asking if he might help, when he gets to high school, turns into a thug who asks if his teacher would like a good poke in the nose. Would he like it now or after school? Here or outside? How about both?

One, for example, was actually in his twenties and so older than some of his teachers. Year after year he deliberately flunked all his courses. For he planned to make a lifetime career out of going to high school. He would walk down the hall of the high school in bare feet, with no shirt on, smoking a cigar. Oddly enough, at such times neither the principal nor the vice-principal could ever be found.

When his parents suggested that he go to work, he beat them senseless. What was so glorious about working with a person like that?

Now, instead of claiming that all of the teaching talent was crowded up at the high school—and all of the incompetence down in the elementaries—our teachers believed that a little more reasonable statement would be that there were some quality people at both levels.

7

At the end of one school year I decided to seize one more of those golden opportunities available to teachers—and to few other men—a chance to go back to school. Right in the middle of his life, teaching offers a man a chance to re-educate himself. He need not feel out of place in a college classroom. If he studies education, he might find that many of the pupils are teachers his own age or even older.

Soon I began to notice that a number of other teachers were also continuing their educations. Two were even working on doctor's degrees.

What connection, I wondered, was there between all this course-taking and a teacher's reputation? I questioned many teachers and I recalled several conversations I had overheard at Pleasant Avenue.

Very little connection, the majority of our teachers agreed. Indeed, nothing was commoner than to hear a teacher remark that some of the best instructors he had ever known had the most modest of educations. And, conversely, some of the worst had the most degrees.

Most teachers took these courses strictly for salary increase purposes. The Pleasant Valley School District gave any teacher $200-a-year more for every fifteen hours of college credits.

Of course, there was a minority opinion. Some people believed that they had profited by their college experiences.

Still, the prevailing opinion was that, as far as helping teach school was concerned, college had been a complete waste of time.

The college from which you had been graduated didn't make any difference either. It would be convenient to state here that, long before any new teacher reported to Pleasant Avenue, his reputation had been already fixed by the college he had attended. This college would either lend some of its own prestige. Or it would give some of its own second-class reputation–which would guarantee the new teacher a second-class life ever after.

But nothing of the kind occurred. The question so often posed to new college teachers, "Where did you take your degree?" would not be heard once in a lifetime at Pleasant Avenue.

Why? Well, to begin with, most of us had attended humdrum colleges of the type one wants to forget–not talk about. Most came from small religious schools where you were graded mainly on your holiness, aggie colleges no one ever heard of before, and teacher colleges that serve only the nearby area and are unheard of five miles away. This is the kind of school where the teacher of creative writing has never published a story or article in his life, and probably never will. This is also kind of fun school in which some students rushes into a classroom and shouts: "Aren't you going to the big rally?" and the whole brainless class marches out the door–without bothering to ask which big rally.

Besides, it kept happening that the teachers who came from such colleges did just fine, but some who came from well-known institutions failed miserably. One of the three who had come from a first-class institution (Berkeley) actually had to be discharged at the end of his second year. Many of us had thought he would up the standards, give our school style. What a mistake! It soon developed that he absolutely could not control children. Apparently passing college courses is one thing, and keeping control in a sixth grade classroom is something else.

His replacement, a staple product from off the shelves

of a nearby engineering school, did just fine. He weighed 225 pounds and was so tough that, when he yelled at the pupils, the teachers who overheard him became afraid.

All our administrators, incidentally, came from undistinguished colleges. Indeed, nothing was commoner in Pleasant Valley than to see graduates of first-class colleges taking orders from administrators who had gone to schools with godforsaken names, such as the University of North Dakota, and who admitted that they had difficulty understanding Donald Duck comic books.

A few teachers practiced a kind of reverse snobbism. They boasted that their second-class educations had prepared them rather well to work in a second-class district. They said that Berkeley, Chicago, and Columbia prepared one to work mainly in such ritzy districts as Beverly Hills, Evanston, or Scarsdale. But not here. Education at such quality colleges might incapacitate one for work in Pleasant Valley. It gave one standards and expectations that would always be inappropriate in Pleasant Valley.

Not realizing that we practiced this kind of snobbism in reverse, one new teacher on arriving at Pleasant Valley told friends that he feared that California teachers might look down on him. After all, he had only a B.A. degree from a small college in Nebraska. He thought we were all graduates of big-time California universities that had national, and even international reputations. No doubt he was afraid at first.

To correct his imaginary deficency, he spent several summer earning a master's degree from Stanford. He thought this would make him more socially acceptable.

Strangely enough, just the opposite occurred. Because now some of the teachers thought of him as a threat to their esteem. Where they had accepted him before, they now wanted nothing to do with him. "The graduates of Black Hills Teacher College or Slippery Rock may not realize it," commented one man. "but a cheery welcome awaits them in almost any faculty lounge in this land. The residents there would be delighted to be compared with them."

Besides, rumor had it that much attendance at colleges

such as Berkeley, Chicago, Harvard, and Columbia had the unfortunate side effect of turning a teacher into too original a thinker—and so possibly into a trouble-maker. I heard teachers say that some superintendents in the area refuse to hire Teachers College, Columbia, graduates, thinking they had been tainted by modernism, Deweyism, and perhaps even Communism.

These men much preferred to hire the docile products turned out by small teacher and religious colleges in the area—the kind of colleges they, themselves, had attended. Such graduates, one teacher explained, were believed to be pure, undefiled, and much easier to control. They had never entertained a dangerous thought in their lives, and were a threat to no one.

Next, consider college degrees. The idea that degrees contribute to teacher quality has been so embedded in salary schedules and popular belief that no one questions it any more. It's an accepted fact. You read in the morning paper that such-and-such a per cent of local teachers have a master's degree. And you say, "My God, isn't it wonderful! Next thing you know, they'll require a bachelor's degree for ditch-diggers and bartenders."

But teachers do not talk this way. Instead, they talk the other way around. A typical Pleasant Avenue teacher would say, "It does not require any Master's degree to teach a kid to read and write." The university, with its obligation to turn out original thought, might require advanced degrees, but not an elementary school. An elementary school is a mass production plant, obligated to put a minimum amount of knowledge in a maximum number of heads. Any education beyond, say the bachelor's degree, would not have much influence on teaching efficiency. In fact, it would be difficult to prove that any education at all affected a teacher's quality. Either a man is a born teacher or he is not. At least, our teachers thought so.

Besides, some powerful people in our system, who influenced the opinions of many others, saw all well-educated teachers as a threat to their own security. Our principal, for example, had never bothered to get a master's degree. He did not pretend to rule by reason of knowing more about this profession than the teachers. Jack claimed that he possessed an inherent superiority, and that we possessed an inherent inferiority, which no amount of education could ever correct. None of our older teachers had master's degrees.

Meanwhile, under the impetus of a very high salary schedule, our school kept filling up with well-educated people. Most had master's degrees, and many had several hours beyond. One actually had 105 hours beyond the master's.

The principal and many older teachers ridiculed these excellent young people. Once, at a faculty meeting, a young man, who happened to be one of the doctoral candidates, made the mistake of mentioning a certain study. He tried to explain the experiments Skinner made with his pigeons. Immediately, two of the older men began to clown. One picked up a BB gun, which for some unknown reason always lay on the floor of our lounge. He began to play at shooting the other, who kept falling out of his chair. Someone else pretended that he could not hear the speaker. He asked one dumbbell question after another. The young man finally got the point. He never brought up a scholarly topic again, knowing full well no one was interested.

Then, too, some of the best educated people had not worked out well in Pleasant Valley. The doctor's degree, so often presumed to be a union card, entitling the holder to an administrative job, had proved to be no such thing in Pleasant Valley. During the period of this study, there were three holders of doctor's degrees on our faculty, all as central office administrators. None lasted more than two years. All experienced continual trouble with other administrators, teachers, and townspeople.

One teacher explained that the reason was the Ph.D. or D. Ed. made these men too much unlike their associates. Doctor's degree holders worked out better in wealthier communities. There, where the teachers are all well-educated and most of the townspeople college graduates, the Ph.D. holder is not so far removed from everyone, as he is in a lower middle class community such as Pleasant Valley.

In general, the teachers thought any Ph.D. in a public school a kind of odd bird who had flown way off his course. We strongly suspected that he had been thrown out of some college faculty or other. Maybe this was right, but the matter was never investigated.

What about college grades? The teachers I talked to (and I assure you I talked to them all) said grades have no conceivable connection with teacher quality either. Indeed, it was fashionable to boast about the number of college courses you had flunked. The champion in this area won his title by announcing that in the small religious college he had attended, he had actually failed religion, traditionally the easiest subject in any church-related college! On the final examination, it seems, he could not even name the Ten Commandments. Yet, even this embarrassing disclosure did not cause him to lose any esteem that I could notice.

And what about those courses a teacher takes which tell him how to teach school? In our time a surprising number of writers criticized them. Our people agreed with every one of these critics. For most of us considered all Education courses pretty worthless.

The main criticism centered on the poverty of their intellectual content. They were so much alike. If you had taken one, the saying went, you had taken them all. Besides, they were so easy to pass that you could not possibly respect them. They offered no challenge.

A number of men commented that they never read their Education texts. No need to. For their professors followed the quaint custom of giving all teachers at least a B. One man told of an extreme case in which a student had left the state in March, yet still received his automatic B in June. People who died in April had no difficulty passing the final exam in June—because there was no final exam. I could not help thinking that the public schoolteacher's traditional low opinion of self might stem from this sensationally easy entry process.

One year our lazy school secretary, Tillie, announced

that she had signed up for a few Education courses, given evenings by a nearby college. These did not prove any great burden. For, she explained, most of the content of the courses consisted of just general information that every housewife and pool player already knew anyway.

In order to get an education, our teachers had majored in such subjects as political science, economics, and English. Anything, except Education!

Another criticism was that Education courses were so impractical. "Once you go to your first job," went the frequently repeated saying, "you can forget everything you ever heard in an Ed. course, because you'll never use any of it. None of it will help you. You're on your own, brother."

"Self-realization. Human relationships. Economic efficiency," said one lovely lady. "Only a college professor could love terms like those. Such phrases are their stock-in-trade. They make their living from them. However, these are good only in a college classroom. They won't help you to survive in the blackboard jungle."

"If you used the term meaningful a lot," said one young girl, "they liked that. I think it helped your grades."

"Yes," said another. "and the word correlated was another of their favorites. They liked that, too. Oh, we know the favorite words by heart."

Some of our teachers did not have such a high opinion of the people they met in these Education courses either. The sensationally easy-to-pass courses, it seems, attract many not overly in love with work, and some of these are not very attractive people. One very beautiful young lady said that back at the sorority house she had been ashamed to admit that she studied with some of these Ed. majors.

She explained that many of these people were the waste products thrown out by other colleges of the university. Flunked out of the medical school, the law school, or even the business school, these rejects found a welcome and even some success in the School of Education. "You see a man walking around the campus, always with his hands in his pockets," she said. "And you wonder why he never carries any books. So one day you ask him if he studies at this university, and he replies, 'No, I'm an Ed. major!'"

For the professors of these despicable Education courses, we reserved a special contempt. Why should we hate these undemanding people who had so courteously allowed us to loaf through four of the best years of our lives?

Part of the reason might be that few of us had ever met a really good professor of Education. We had attended very small schools, where the so-called Education Department consisted of only one or two teachers. These poverty-stricken little schools never had enough money to attract even one first-class teacher. Many paid less than the local public schools.

Oh, the unkind stories that were told about these poor Education professors. "I remember one course I took in how to teach English," said one man. "All the course consisted of was this fellow, complete with phony English accent, reading the works of his favorite poets, and we students enjoying it. He really took it easy on us, which at the time we appreciated. He probably did develop in some of us hayshakers a love for poetry. However, when we got out on the job, we discovered that there is a lot more to the teaching of English than the appreciation of poetry—and we simply didn't know that lot more."

I once had an argument with one of our teachers. I had recently had the honor of taking a summer school course at Harvard from a very great educator, Herold Hunt. Now, Dr. Hunt was at one time General Superintendent of Schools of Chicago and at another time Assistant Secretary of Health, Education and Welfare. "Wasn't it possible," I asked, "that Dr. Hunt could have something valuable to say to even the most experienced classroom teacher?"

"No," replied this middle-aged man. "All Education teachers are just damned fools." This man simply could not imagine an Education professor as anything except a broken-down comedian who read the same lectures year after year, and made a salary lower than that of a kindergarten teacher. Most of the other teachers in the lounge nodded in agreement and that settled that.

Well, if the Pleasant Avenue teacher did not learn much about teaching back at college, then how did he learn how to teach? The answer, if I interpret the conversations of our teachers correctly, is he taught himself. And other teachers taught him.

The more-or-less typical new teacher came to Pleasant Valley with a headfull of textbook generalizations and youthful idealism. Some of the generalizations did not have much to do with local problems and so were forgotten after the first week or so. Some of the idealism did not last through the first day.

"Instead of the kids in my class being all on one reading level," groaned one lady, "I just found that mine read all the way from second grade clear up to someplace in high school." One young man, preparing to do a unit on the United Nations, found that some of his fifth grade pupils could not even read.

While going through one jolting experience after another, the new Pleasant Avenue teacher, if he survived, finally learned what qualities were necessary for success in our particular school.

8

Rather often, during the time I spent at Pleasant Avenue, there were comments by parents and other townspeople to the effect that the old-time teacher was more dedicated than the modern one. They said that a kind of religious zeal drove the typical teacher of long ago. And, as a matter of fact, quite a few of them were the daughters of ministers.

This teacher did not work for mere money. All she wanted out of life was to direct young lives in the way they should go, to make a little culture and refinement bloom in a spiritually and culturally arid community. She did not care what hours she worked either. In fact, she thought so little of the things of this world that she did not even bother to get married. When she retired, plenty of people said they were better men and women today because long ago she had done way more for them than she was required to.

But the modern teacher, so the story went (who was as likely as not the brother or son of a member of the A.F. of L.), all too often regarded his work as a strictly nine to five proposition–a portal to portal sort of thing. He was interested mainly in wages and hours.

I do not know how dedicated the oldtime school teachers were, but I think it a little unlikely that every one of them was a consecrated saint. I do know, however, that no one at Pleasant Avenue could ever get the reputation of a good teacher if he lacked interest in the welfare of the children.

Delivering a lecture with a take-it-or-leave-it attitude might do at the university level. There, a professor may read a lecture in a bored voice or even just read the textbook. Meanwhile, some of the pupils sit there reading newspapers.

Such work standards would never get the approval of Pleasant Avenue teachers. If you were to look in the doorway of one teacher whom other teachers admired you might see him standing over some dense and bored pupil, patiently explaining the same simple facts over and over again. Then you would see him turn around to reprimand some lazy pupil who was wasting his time drawing pictures of horses, when he should have been working problems in long division. After that he might rush to the opposite end of the room to calm down one of the budding comedians, of which our school had an unlimited supply.

Next he might stop by a desk to ask some little girl why she was not producing any more. She used to be such a good student. Was there something wrong at home? Was she feeling well? Better call in the mother for a conference.

If you walked down the hall on a typical day, you would see this teacher standing there having a heart-to-heart talk with some pupil. "Look, Bob, you have it in you to some day become a mighty nice person, but you must do something about this laziness." "Remember, Jack, that more than one good person has been ruined by his temper. Learn to control it."

Incidentally, this business of correcting not only the grammar and mathematics of the children, but also their manners and ethics can be fatiguing. For many a pupil is bound and determined to go wrong in life. And a teacher must work long and hard to correct him and get him back on the right track.

Furthermore, not only was the teacher that other teachers admired devoted to the children but also he was intensely loyal to all fellow-teachers–and that whether or not he happened to like or approve of some of them. Thus, when discussing the faculty with anyone except an intimate friend, the good Pleasant Avenue teacher spoke somewhat as follows:

"This is absolutely the best bunch of teachers in the entire world! What wild, impossible magic brought so many excellent teachers into just one school? Will you tell me that? I've taught in one or two schools in my day, but, believe, me, this faculty beats them all. The best–the very best!"

As further social insurance, the good teacher not only sang the praises of the faculty as a group, but of all individuals in it as well. Thus, when discussing the most worthless teacher on the staff, the good teacher would speak somewhat as follows: "That third grade teacher down the hall! I'm crazy about her. The way she handles a class! Boy, she's great. The best!"

One day I asked one of our teachers whom all the others called good if he had heard what had become of a former colleague. We both knew that this man had been fired in Pleasant Valley. Immediately jumping to his defense of this talentless man, the good teacher replied. "Oh, Johnny has a good job now. He's in city management." He went on to explain that this complete no-good now worked as a clerk in the office of the water commissioner in another town.

Several times parents asked me whether or not their son or daughter had a good teacher this year. I remember more than once feeling tempted to say that this one or that had the world's worst fraud. But I resisted the temptation and always replied that the teacher in question was a gem, a wonderful person. Simply marvelous. What else could I say? We stuck together, for better or worse.

In fact, the merest hint that you were having trouble with another teacher could get you into serious trouble. Our principal once severely criticized a young lady for fighting with another teacher. But, she protested, she had not said one word to the other woman.

"That's true." the principal replied.

"Well, then," this teacher asked, "what have I done that is so wrong?"

"Well, when two other teachers made derogatory remarks about her, you *listened*."

Next, the good teacher was absolutely dedicated to this

profession. One year, when I asked all 98 past and present faculty members if they considered elementary teaching a profession in the same class with law and medicine, all but 14 said certainly it was. Two said they considered teaching more important than law or medicine. Even the two sweet little old ladies who had never bothered to graduate from college said they felt that they were just as professional as any doctor or lawyer in this world.

A good way to commit social suicide would be to say something against the profession of teaching. For example, if you said that in any occupation where the members do not get paid much in money, they frequently try to take their pay home in the form of glory–that would make our teachers extremely angry.

However, though we stoutly maintained that this definitely is a profession, that does not mean that we called all in it professionals. Far from it. When our teachers described a colleague they particularly admired they called him a "professional." They spoke this way to differentiate him from other teachers whom they considered less than professional. These they called unprofessional.

For one teacher to call another unprofessional was absolutely the worst thing he could say. It deeply hurt feelings. Because all teachers want the reputation of professional or good teachers. Incidentally, by manipulating good opinion, by conferring or withholding esteem in this way, teachers do a better job of policing their own ranks than many people realize.

Another way you could tell a good teacher, our teachers believed, was by how much he loved this profession. I once asked every teacher past and present the question, "why did you become a teacher?" It seemed to me that each wracked his brains to find superlatives to describe his love for the work. I don't think they felt obligated to give stock answers which would sound good either. For most of them were personal friends whom I had known for years. I believe they told the truth.

I was considerably surprised to get replies such as these:

"I can't remember when I didn't want to teach." "I always ranked it as the highest profession." "This is all I ever wanted to do all my life." Two would not tell. They said the reasons were too sacred to mention in public.

On only two occasions did I hear teachers criticize the profession. Both times other teachers severely criticized them. The principal had to transfer one man out of the building, though he probably made other mistakes too.

What about membership in professional societies, traditionally supposed to be the hallmark of any good teacher? Our teachers were split into two groups. One group believed that any good teacher would certainly join local, state, and national societies. Year after year they went around to the different rooms urging others to join. But only about half of us lethargically made out checks, then forgot all about the associations.

Since we were treated pretty well, there was not much need for an association. We were different from the teachers in districts where the teachers continually fight with the school board and the community. There every teachers owes his job—and maybe even his life—to the local teachers' association or to the teachers' union. In our district much job security produced much contentment; and the great majority of our teachers did not see professional membership as outward evidence of inward quality in a teacher.

A name that did come up rather often in our lounge was that of the teachers' union, the A.F.T. Before the New York City Teachers' strike of April 11, 1961, most did not even know there was an American Federation of Teachers. After the strike, they talked of nothing else. However, they talked in hushed voices. The union question was very controversial. The superintendent and many of the principals were wildly against it. They knew it meant more power for teachers (such as power to dictate their own working conditions), the end of much of their power to control teachers (who are pretty independent as it is), and so the beginning of many new headaches for them.

It was mainly young married men who praised the union.

They said it was the wave of the future, bringing better working conditions, better salaries– and so attracting better people into the profession. This, they said, would not only improve the quality of the education the children received, but also add to public respect for teachers.

"No. That's where you are wrong," shouted one of the elderly married ladies who always opposed everything new, no matter what it was. "Teachers are professionals, and professionals are not supposed to join unions. If teachers join unions, the public will think no more of them than they do of bricklayers. A good teacher would not join a union."

That day I saw for the first time a phenomenon which I was to see rather often afterwards: teachers who belonged to the working class economically, still remaining bitterly anti-working class in sentiment. They reminded me of the last stragglers of some departing era. They were like a decaying aristocracy who had difficulty adjusting to life in a new republic.

A third opinion, and one a little more reasonable, was expressed by our principal. He said, "Some good teachers, belong to unions. And some good ones do not."

Fortunately the union question never came up for a vote in our school. For one reason, the union organizers were so busy signing up teachers in the district around us (where they were colossally successful) that they never got around to us. Meanwhile, the great debate in our faculty lounge went on and on.

Were there any other ways teachers assessed each others' competency? I walked back to the gym taking notes on the conversations I had just overheard in the lounge.

9

The teacher, we know, handles not merely goods or money, but the lives of little children. He attempts to pass along, not just information, but also ideals, values, traditions. Thus, our teachers believed, the necessity of his being a person of the highest moral character.

All Pleasant Avenue teachers I ever heard mention the subject (and this study is based mainly on overheard conversations) agreed that moral character ranked above love of children, desire to teach, intelligence, or anything else in the make-up of a good teacher. There was no compromise nor minority opinion on this issue. We felt and spoke as one. In fact, that stock character, the old maid schoolteacher of a generation or two ago, who wore out the church door, never touched spiritous liquors as far as anyone knew, and never had a date in her life, would have fitted in just fine on our faculty.

To show what I mean by morality here are examples from just two areas: Sex and church membership. However, there is more to faculty morality than these. I include these only to illustrate my point that the good teacher at Pleasant Avenue at least, was the most moral person this side of the angels.

To begin with, sometimes one hears people of a nasty disposition say that teachers (especially women teachers) have loose morals. They say that teachers are so inhibited by the nature of their work that once they get outside the building, they go hog wild and kick up their heels. All they want to do is screw. They can't get enough. According to one story, every time the teachers throw a party, the neighbors have to come in and pour hot water on them to get them apart.

I do not believe such ridiculous stories. On the contrary, my experiences at Pleasant Avenue convinced me that most public school teachers are not only moral, but also positively puritanical. Maybe some old-maid schoolteacher a generation or so ago did go to hotel rooms with salesmen, this being as close to romance as the poor thing would ever get. But the modern teacher is a very happily married woman. Salesmen do not interest her in the least.

Most of our teachers, including those in their early 20's were old married homebodys who would bore you stiff talking about their children, their homes, their boats, and their gardens. Teacher marriages, by the way, have for years been world famous for their stability. At the business of running decent and happy homes, only ministers of the gospel beat public schoolteachers.

Whether married or not, moreover, teachers live according to the highest of moral principles. I know of only one great lover who overstepped the bounds. She worked in another school in our system. Our teachers did not consider her a morals case; they called her a mental case.

It seems a middle-aged business man was dating this lush, blonde physical education teacher. Here he was a married man with children. And she suddenly announced their engagement.

Though our teachers usually laughed at all stories about dalliance, none laughed at this one involving a teacher. The fact that this girl had great skill at teaching meant nothing now. All teachers wanted her off the payroll immediately. Two men considered the affair too disgusting even to talk about.

The subject of church membership is a complicated one. Years ago, old residents say, every teacher was required to attend some church or other, no matter what. They had to be seen. Many taught Sunday school. Naturally, the principal took up the collection, that being the most important and conspicuous position, except that of the minister himself.

By the 1960's, however, nobody cared if you went to church or not. That was entirely your own business. School district regulations said nothing about either church membership or attendance. Most of our teachers called this a great blessing.

Of course, fewer teachers went to church. Only about half were church members. And I strongly suspect some of these were not very active. Some made no secret of the fact that they were atheists. Others joked that they had long ago been excommunicated. And still nobody cared. Religion was simply not a topic worth arguing over.

All of which does not mean, however, that religion had no place in our lives. It had. We talked continually about what is right and what is wrong. A teacher, remember, spends a lifetime telling children not to cheat on tests, not to steal from each other, and not to strike each other. After a while, he gets to be pretty discriminating on this subject.

However, our teachers did not see much connection between this and church membership. We believed a person can live a perfectly ethical life without bothering to go to church at all. One time in the faculty lounge I tried to describe a teacher I particularly admired. By the way of proving his quality, I mentioned that he was a member of the Methodist Church. Several of the men burst out laughing. "What connection," someone asked, "does psalm-singing have with good teaching?"

Membership in semi-religious lodges did not seem to have much influence with our teachers, either. In college, I heard that if you joined some lodge, such as the Masons or Knights of Columbus, it would do your career no harm.

This advice may be absolutely true. But you could not prove it at Pleasant Avenue. There the only talk against one excellent man, who happened to be a Mason, all came from another Mason. Who stuck up for him? All the Roman Catholics in the building. And conversely, the worst criticism of one Irish Catholic administrator all seemed to come from other Irish Catholics.

And now for a word about our ethics when dealing with our employer, The Pleasant Valley Unified School District. As you probably already suspect, the teachers' teacher, the one admired by others, was always a very hard worker. In the cafeteria, I once saw a man doing three things at once. He ate his lunch, corrected papers, and kept order among the children–all at the same time. He would stuff those delicious surplus powdered eggs into his mouth, make a few check marks on a child's paper, then jump up and run to the opposite end of the room to restore order. Many people called this man the best teacher in the history of our school.

Of course, human nature being what it is, we had a few not excessively dedicated too. One, for example, used to give a test that would take up the time of the children, then throw the results in the waste basket, thus saving herself the trouble of correcting them.

Another had the habit of throwing the children's homework in the waste basket too, thus saving himself the labor of correcting it. So many did this that the parents began to complain to the superintendent. They insisted that all homework be returned to the children. Then the parents checked on the teachers' corrections, thus ruining all of the fun.

We often laughed among ourselves about the bulging briefcases we carried home each afternoon. For we knew that some contained nothing but old newspapers. School district regulations said that all teachers had to take home some papers to correct. Taxpayers like to believe that teachers work both day and night. So some teachers happily supplied the illusion.

One man employed the interesting and labor-saving technique of priming the class. Just before a big examination he would shoot the classmembers full of knowledge on one particular subject. Or he would brief his pupils on the questions that would appear on the exam. Thus, even a student who had not been taught much during the year could still pass. However, such people were definitely not the Pleasant Avenue teachers' idea of a good teacher.

Yet, strange as it may sound, even they had their value. For the principal usually assigned them to classes no one else wanted. I suppose all schools keep a few non-productive faculty members around–in order to do the work no one else wants to do.

"Let's get some real producers in this district," taxpayers often cried, especially at wild public meetings. Apparently they did not realize that first-class teachers are often uninclined to teach some of the dull or disruptive pupils we had. The good teacher, perhaps realizing his own quality, often insists on and gets first-class pupils. These taxpayers did not understand that the only reason some of their children had any teachers at all was that there were mediocrities on our staff.

And so ended the first year of my attempt to find how teachers appraise the quality of other teachers.

10

Constantly during the period of this study, parents exclaimed that modern teachers have at their disposal such a wealth of new teaching and (expensive) equipment. Each wanted to know if his child's teacher employed these new techniques. The general opinion was that any good teacher would.

However, again Pleasant Avenue teachers did not speak this way. They said that many of these innovations did not make much difference one way or the other.

For example, we heard that the progressive teacher controls pupils by employing the principles of psychology, a subject he knows all about, of course. Always being careful not to wound young egos, he subtly motivates all pupils to do as he wishes. Why, he never even raises his voice. No need to.

"Now children, come to order!" he says in a calm voice. "If you *please,* Richard!" he adds to one wretch, who of course immediately turns into an adjusted and cooperative little gentleman. "All right, now let's open our social studies books to page 109."

In some schools this picture may be true. However, one hundred per cent of our teachers achieved control by simply yelling at the kids the way cowboys out West holler at cattle. "Will you shut up that mouth of *yours,*" a more-or-less typical teacher would shout. He was talking to a darling little girl who went around telling other children to be quiet–yet did more talking than anyone else in the building.

"What do you mean, 'Why are we studying the Emancipation Proclamation?' Because it's Tuesday, that's why."

The big argument over whether children learn more under democratic or authoritarian teachers never entered our heads. In our school the idea of a permissive classroom atmosphere–so often associated with the progressive education movement fell into complete disgrace. The old idea that a teacher should help the pupil with his emotional problems (and not just his intellectual ones) went out the window.

The teacher who was admired, the teacher's teacher, was a no-nonsense type who bawled hell out of the kids from morning until night. Strong teacher meant good teacher. Ex-bartenders, ex-army sergeants, and ex-prison guards found a ready welcome among us. They knew the ropes. Many of our men remarked in amazement that, while the education they received in college proved worse than useless, the things they learned about handling men in the infantry came in mighty handy. Quite a few called their classes to order by shouting: "TEN-SHUN!" Strangely this seemed to work, and those kids obeyed on the double.

This might have been called the day of the ruination of the man of culture and refinement, and the day of the glorification of the bum who happened to have gone to college.

It would be indeed difficult to overemphasize the importance placed on this ability to handle a class. If you had it, you had job security, good reputation, everything. If you did not have it, you could not even stay on the payroll.

Here is a typical teacher's description of a good teacher. "Smith picked up this boy–and threw him across two desks. The kid hit the wall and dropped to the floor. From that day on, the kid was a different person. No more trouble. Talk about making changes in behavior–as the nuts back at the university call it. Smith really had it. This kid grew to love him. After that, Smith could hardly get rid of him. As far as I know, the kid still writes letters to him.

"Naturally, a teacher who can control pupils like that

can also write his own contract in any school district. Wouldn't you know it? Another district grabbed him. Offered him more money. It's very difficult to keep a quality teacher like Smith."

Even teachers who were physically repulsive or downright unintelligent, still enjoyed excellent reputations within the teacher group if they could keep order. For that was very nearly all that was asked.

Now comes the question, "What kind of people kept the best order?" One might think that tall and powerfully-built men kept the best. But again, nothing of the kind occurred. What kind of teacher kept the best order? All kinds! Tall. short, skinny, fat, young, old, male, female, both, neither.

One year, a man six feet six, weighing around two hundred and fifty pounds, joined the staff. When the principal introduced him at the first staff meeting, all the teachers burst into spontaneous applause. Now here was the teachers' idea of a good teacher–a fracturer. We soon discovered, however, that we had made a mistake. This man had no fight in him. And, since he did not dominate his pupils, they tortured him instead, as is usual.

At the opposite extreme, one frail little lady in her early twenties, and weighing not over one hundred pounds, kept perfect order. This she accomplished by tongue-lashing her pupils continually. Yet she did not dislike children. She simply was a very strong and a very stern person who had high standards.

Strangely, the students loved her. They much preferred her to a very kindly man who taught them the year before and had taken it easy on them. "May I go to the bathroom?" a typical boy would ask him. When he replied no, the boy used to thank him and walk out the door anyway. This was not out of impoliteness but because none of the pupils ever paid any attention to anything he said.

One day the New Math suddenly came to Pleasant Avenue. And the superintendent, who had had much experience at handling teachers, announced diplomatically that those who wished to teach by that method could do so, and those who wished to teach old math could do that too. You might think that shortly thereafter our faculty would divide into ossified defenders of old math, on the one hand, and eager young advocates of modern math on the other.

But nothing of the kind occurred. One day another teacher and I were listening to the pupils in one classroom reciting the multiplication tables in a sing-song fashion. I remarked that that was the way they taught math when I was a child. "That's the way children learned to multiply in my father's day," the other teacher replied. "I know because I asked him last night." Yet this teacher and every other one in the building admitted that the man who used this old method was one of our best.

Next this teacher and I began to discuss the Cuisenaire Rods and other devices used in teaching modern math. Several teachers present mentioned the poor results some of the teachers who taught modern math were getting. No, someone said, you could not tell a teacher's quality from the way he taught arithmetic—or any other subject.

Sometimes, in a store window downtown or in a newspaper photograph, you see fascinating examples of childrens' school work. Here is a dry cell battery sawed down the middle and a crudely printed explanation of how it works. There are several crayons pasted to a piece of cardboard, along with the child's printed explanation that this exhibit explains how crayons act as crayons.

And over there is a newspaper completely written by fifth graders. One news item proposes three cheers for the very superior work of our janitor. Another thanks the cafeteria ladies for dedicating their lives to the school.

Sometimes, people outside the profession give special admiration to the teachers of such children. They say, "Now here is someone doing something more than just assigning so many pages from the textbook." It does seem that all a teacher would need to do to transform himself into a good one would be to involve his pupils in such interesting activities.

At Pleasant Avenue, however, we did not think this way. We did not believe that activities signalized either the presence or absence of quality teaching.

One woman once allowed her pupils to build a house of cardboard right in the classroom. For weeks, the kids sawed and hammered–and incidentally learned a lot of math while taking measurements, and a lot of English while writing away for supplies.

By the time it was completed, the children were beside themselves with happiness–and the teacher was a physical wreck. Teachers who came in to look pronounced this a very valuable learning experience.

However, nobody claimed that this woman was any better than the man at the opposite end of the hall who did not involve his students in any kind of activities at all. There were no examples of the children's art work on the windows of his classroom–which might proclaim his quality to the world. There were no examples of the children's homework on the wall outside his classroom either. He never took his students on any field trips. All he ever did was drill the hell out of them. But he got good results. And so he too enjoyed the reputation of an excellent schoolman.

Indeed, one teacher said that if he saw all kinds of exhibits and art work over the walls inside and outside a certain classroom, he might become a little suspicious. Because he might wonder what on earth the children could possibly learn while drawing so many pictures. He might remember that tired, overworked, or just unambitious teachers often direct their pupils to draw many pretty pictures–while they take a much-needed rest. Such exhibits, therefore, far from signalling the presence of a good teacher, might actually signal the presence of something else.

In former days, the only equipment a classroom contained was a wall map and a picture of George Washington. But later the average classroom began to fill up with more and more electrical equipment. For many an enterprising businessman had discovered that the parents, in their quest for quality education, would buy anything that looked like it would give a better education to their children.

Why certainly, I once heard a salesman say. All you did was plug in this contraption. If it happened to be working that day, it immediately turned the most dense and disruptive pupil into a very intelligent and saintly individual. Now the cost of this model was only $3,000. The home office had only a few thousand left and the price was due to go up next month. So shouldn't you place an order immediately? All progressive teachers used them.

But again, you did not hear teachers talk this way. Instead they were a little inclined to suspect some of this miracle-working machinery. At a teacher's meeting, at which a salesman explained to us the miracles computers could accomplish, one teacher in a low voice asked those of us at our table how come Socrates and Jesus managed to get by on just the lecture method of teaching. Were they stupid? "Imagine," he said, "the carelessness of God the Father, handing out those Ten Commandments on two tablets of stone. Why didn't he hand them out on IBM cards, instead?"

Besides some of our people had gone through some pretty disillusioning experiences with some of these new teaching devices. For example, one of the women teachers more than once remarked that not all children did such a good job of education themselves in those new carrels. They were supposed to sit there, viewing films and listening to tapes and records. No teacher needed.

She happened to notice that some mischievous children, for diversion, were showing the films upside down, on the ceiling, or even on their friends' foreheads.

When one new superintendent installed television sets in each classroom many of us expected this to revolutionize schoolteaching in our little school. Now the children could watch master teachers demonstrating with expensive equipment, see newsreels of history as it really happened, and listen to the speeches of great men such as Winston Churchill.

In practice, however, these sets did not accomplish any such wild, impossible magic. True, teachers did occasionally comment that their class had seen a good film. In general, however, our teachers tended to leave the sets off.

One teacher explained that the films never had much to do with what went on in the classrooms. Therefore, about the only way teachers could use this new teaching device was for entertainment. For example, a teacher whose class had grown tired of studying the Civil War might switch on the set–and the class would watch a film on the manufacture of cement. But that was about all.

No, our teachers agreed, you cannot tell much about a teacher's quality from the methods he uses, nor from his use or non-use of teaching hardware either.

11

Over the years I settled into a beautiful routine in Pleasant Valley. Before driving to school each morning, I ate breakfast at a nearby drug store, and I got to know the lady who ran the lunch counter. She was the all-business, no-nonsense type of person I always admired so much.

She had, incidentally, her own way of judging teacher quality. She judged teachers by their families. That is, she asked what your father, your uncles, and your cousins did for a living. If you replied that they were all business and professional men, she said that meant you were a good teacher.

This lady often talked about Pleasant Avenue teachers she liked and considered outstanding. And she mentioned a few she did not like, too. As I sat there every morning eating fried eggs, bacon, toast and marmalade, I enjoyed talking with her about the various teachers we considered outstanding. But I kept pretty quiet about the innefficient ones.

Later, as I drove to work, I could not help thinking about this relationship between popularity and teaching efficiency. Every year, we see in novels, motion pictures, and television shows, teachers beloved by parents, fellow-teachers, or students. It is interesting to ask if these teachers, beloved by different groups, are the teachers' idea of good teachers.

At Pleasant Avenue we said that much depends on whom the popularity is with. Popularity with teachers or pupils does have some significance. Popularity with parents or other townspeople, however, signifies very little. In fact, we believed that the educational world is divided into two classes: the teachers and the children who know everything about it–and the parents and other outsiders who know nothing.

Let's look a little more at the teacher who is popular with other teachers. Approximately once a year you read in the newspaper that a teacher has been elected to office in some teachers' association. You wonder if this teacher, so obviously popular with colleagues, is also pretty good in the classroom. Is he or isn't he? The answer at Pleasant Avenue was, he is.

Of course, a number of good teachers did not care to go to the boring teachers' association meetings, and as a result, did not get elected to any office. Still, from the number that did attend, teachers always selected the very best.

Once elected, these teachers' association officers always worked for the best interests of the children, as well as the teachers. Furthermore, every officer did all of his association work after school–and sometimes at considerable personal expense,–money-wise and time-wise.

So much for the office holder. Now what about the teacher who is just plain well-liked–the kind everyone wants to talk to in the faculty lounge? This kind almost invariably had the reputation of being a good teacher too.

But why, someone might ask? Why would the teacher in 211 care what the teacher in 213 did? Well, for one reason, the skillful in almost any occupation is usually admired. For another, a master teacher can often be a great help to others. For teaching, though usually a great pleasure, still at times can become a little difficult too. New forms are always coming out–then getting revised. New orders appear on purple mimeographed sheets–and need to be explained. The wildest rumors shoot through the building–and need to be verified. Women occasionally run into a boy too tough to handle. New electronic equipment can be confusing to understand.

Teachers with such problems often do not wish to expose their ignorance to the principal–who once a year evaluates them. Many, therefore, go to some master teacher who always seems to know how to do every little thing. Every school has a few of these, who, incidentally, do much more work than they ever get paid for. Naturally such outstanding people receive considerable respect.

So much for the good teachers. Now let us consider the incompetents. In general, other teachers shower them with contempt. When, for example, a good teacher retired, we gave him a dinner and a present, such as a wrist watch. The superintendent made a speech. This ceremony assured the good teacher a pleasant memory. For there are not many rewards in life greater than the respect and love of one's colleagues.

But when an incompetent was fired or even retired, we did nothing, nothing at all. I remember one dear old lady who told us that this would be her last year of teaching. Then on the last day of school she went to the lounge and sat down, waiting in that heat for the traditional going-away party. What she did not know was that the teachers had decided not to give her any. Finally two of her friends took her downtown for tea. When she walked out the door, nobody said a thing, Teachers, though usually friendly, can be cruel at times too.

Why the great unpopularity of the incompetent? Why should one teacher care what went on in the room next door? One man told me that when he watched another fumble a class, he thought of the very good possibility that he might inherit those very same pupils the next year. He added that children taught nothing one year can be most difficult to teach the next. For the teacher the second year will have to work extra hard to teach them all they had missed the previous year, plus all they are supposed to learn this one.

Also, children permitted to do as they please one year can be murder to control the next. For in a public school rebellion has a tendency to spread. If the children are allowed to run wild in one classroom, then for some reason, those in the other rooms will try the same thing. If one teacher takes it easy on his kids—allows them to leave the room whenever they like, gives them no homework—then every other kid in the building will expect the same treatment. Soon even the best students are goofing off—or trying to wrest control of the school away from the teachers.

Whatever the reason for the unpopularity of the incompetent, at Pleasant Avenue once professional relationships between two teachers began to deteriorate, personal relationships went to hell too.

Now what about this matter of popularity with students? No doubt you have noticed that children run all over town telling how much they love some teachers—and also how much they hate others. They divulge everything with no inhibitions. They withhold nothing.

Pleasant Avenue kids gave some pretty dramatic demonstrations of their feelings. At Christmas time, for example, when it was traditional for them to bring presents to their teachers, they brought so many to some that these men and women had to carry the loot out to their cars in cartons. Some had to make several trips. These were not expensive gifts, some even homemade, but the children's hearts were in each package.

Some pupils gave their teachers birthday parties. For weeks they assembled signs saying, "We love you," paper streamers, and bags of food. Then one day when the teacher walked in, they all shouted "Surprise," and the party was on.

One group even composed and acted out a 13 act drama (later shortened to 9 acts) to honor their teacher. The plot concerned a fiend who went around strangling people. He lived in a graveyard, and drank human blood. Every now and then he took possession of someone's soul. The pupils, while dining on jelly beans, soda pop, and pickles, pronounced the play a complete success and a fitting gift for the teacher they loved. Though they pretend to be merely amused, teachers who receive parties were usually very grateful, and immediately informed everyone in the building.

Yet, at the same time that some pupils were demonstrating their love for their teachers, others were telling the world how much they hated theirs. On occasion, pupils threw large rocks through the classroom windows of certain teachers.

They pasted the library books together (the library paste being conveniently at hand), and they threw paint against the walls of certain classrooms. Then they squirted lighter fluid into the office filing cabinets, and touched a match to the whole thing.

"Pleasant Valley Pupils Vandalize School," screamed the headline in the newspaper. But one teacher pointed out to another that these pupils had not even touched certain classrooms. They only smashed up the rooms of the teachers they despised.

Our teachers had great respect for the opinions of students concerning the quality of their teachers. We believed that pupils, being in closer contact with their teachers than anyone else, and having the opportunity to observe them for a year at a time, often made amazingly good judgments. Their standards were extremely high. For they were at an age when they were all idealists.

Therefore, some teachers when they wanted to know if a new faculty member was a good one, simply tuned in one of these charmers. These, delighted to show off their intimate knowledge, often made shockingly frank statements.

"What is your teacher doing these days?" I once asked one little boy who spent considerable time in the gym helping me, his teacher being pretty generous about sending him there.

"You want to know what that bum did all morning?" He exclaimed. "She read the morning paper and addressed her Christmas cards."

Now, few teachers would have dared to speak that frankly–or that accurately. No one would have suspected that the old lady in 102 was a goof-off. But it was true. The kids had information that could be obtained from no other source.

As if that were not enough, they were incorruptible. You might think that if a teacher allowed her children to play all day, this alone might purchase much popularity. But no. One gal who was an absolute slave-driver (No parties or trips for her kids. She even kept them in during playground period and drilled them.) was also one of our most popular.

"She really works you hard," said a little girl whom I had previously thought rather dense, "but you learn a lot from her."

Now let's consider teacher popularity with parents and other community members. Some parents rush to enroll their children in the classes of certain teachers. And they scream bloody murder when they find that their children have been assigned to others. How good are these people at judging teacher quality?

Not very good, our teachers said. Parents are too easily fooled by appearances. Nothing is commoner than to see parents falling all over some dumbbell because he has wavy hair, and jumping all over some excellent professional because he works the children so hard.

One year the ladies of the P.T.A. elected a teacher president just a few days before the principal fired him for stupidity–lack of interest in one's work being a form of stupidity. That same year, a father tried hard to get rid of one man we teachers called the best our school ever had.

In fact, there was an opinion among us that one way you could tell a good teacher was by the fact that he occasionally got into trouble with parents. For any good teacher would naturally have opinions contrary to those of the man in the streets. If he had any quality, we said, then his beliefs would have to clash occasionally with those of someone who knew nothing about education.

Conversely, our teachers looked with suspicion at those who enjoyed a superabundance of community popularity. (The quack, remember, is traditionally someone who over-pleases the customers.) Such teachers we usually suspected of taking a short-cut to security.

I don't know why our teachers judged each other in this way. Maybe years of grading students had put them in the habit of grading everything they saw. And, after they got through ruling on the quality of each student every day, they went right on and graded each other as well. Whatever the reason, this was yet another way teachers judged the quality of other teachers in wonderful Pleasant Avenue School.

12

As the years flew by and the work became easier and even more of a pleasure, I began taking an interest in that great phenomenon of public school life–cliques. I noticed, for example, that our faculty, far from being just one big family, was instead several little families.

One of these was composed of some of the principal's loyal followers. They liked the way he did things. He got along with them too. And you often saw him laughing and talking with them.

But what set them off from the other teachers was not just that Jack found their company so pleasurable. What set them apart was that each was an excellent teacher–who could probably never be replaced. And equally important, every one contributed some special talent to the school which the school needed and which no one else could give it. It was, therefore, possible to feel called to this charmed circle, yet never be chosen.

Tom Snow had a special talent. He relieved Jack of one of his most pesky problems–the entertainment one. To amuse members of the public, every school must put on dramas, chorales, and games. Within the profession, we call this the circus side of schoolteaching.

One day, Jack, who was quite a public relations man, thought it might be a good idea if the teachers sponsored one of those comic basketball games. The money could go to charity. This would convince local taxpayers that we teachers were not aloof but instead informal, even a little playful.

Anyway, Jack handed the problem over to Tom, who promptly did a good job of organizing the whole thing. He talked several of the men who were good friends of Jack into putting on goofy costumes. One wore the dress of a ballet dancer. Another dressed as an Indian clad only in a breech cloth. The team we played, the local high school boys, wore no costumes.

Without their neatly pressed suits, some of our men looked pretty ridiculous. Such big rears ends! Such fat bellies! Why, some of them were so overweight from sitting at a desk all day, that when they ran, their breasts bounced up and down. No wonder the audience nearly died laughing.

Naturally, some of the teachers objected. They complained that such shows appealed not to all citizens, but mainly to ones of an unrefined temperament. Such people want to see teachers dragged down off their high social perches. These teachers argued that teachers who put on goofy costumes and run around in public are the sideshow freaks of the profession–every profession having a few members who act in an uncultivated manner.

"That's the spirit," said one of the members of the principal's clique. "You take it easy. God forbid that you should give up one of your evenings doing this sort of thing. Well, it so happens that only a good teacher would do this extra work."

The next clique of importance in the life of a Pleasant Avenue teacher was that of the outsiders, sometimes referred to as the trouble-makers or losers. Just as the principal's clique contained all those who liked the way Jack ran things (and were reputed to be getting all of the goodies), so this one contained those who did not like Jack's methods (and were not getting what they thought their fair share of the prizes of public school life).

Unlike the principal's clique, which was rather exclusive, this one was wide open to anyone. Members carried on an active program of recruitment, especially among new teachers, to convince all that they were miserable and oppressed and should join in this patriotic business of tunnelling and undermining the principal. Their aim was to make his work more difficult–and perhaps eventually drive him out of the school. Their method was speaking against him throughout the school and community.

Often, when a member of this clique met a member of the principal's clique, he made jokes at the other's expense. He kidded about the other's pupils, his teaching methods, or something else. Anything would do. Usually the joke contained some pejorative revelation. Listeners were supposed to get the impression that the victim was a person of less quality than the commentator.

"Oh, Mr. Higgins," a members of this clique said one day to a member of the principal's clique, who at the time was resting in the faculty lounge. "Your children are killing each other in your classroom. Do you want me to go down to restore order? Be glad to. Only take a minute."

Until that moment I had not realized that old man Higgins had the habit of walking out the door of his classroom, leaving his pupils unattended, while he took a rest in the faculty lounge. Definitely he was not a good teacher. I never thought much of him afterwards.

A more or less typical member of this group was a tall, distinguished-looking man in his late 40's, named Bob Kennedy. Bob was the clean-living, familyman type you like to see in schoolteaching. He came from an important California family, and had been born and raised in a community very near Pleasant Valley. One day Bob told us that often as a boy, he and his grandfather had driven down the very superhighway that now ran past Pleasant Avenue School. Only in those days the highway had been just two ruts in a sandy road.

Who would have guessed then that one day he would teach in the little school by the side of that very road? Worse, who would have dreamed that he would work there for someone who came from the other end of the country? Almost unthinkable.

Naturally, Bob felt that if anyone deserved promotion, it was he. Many teachers agreed. This was his locale. He belonged here. Still, Jack, who acted as gate-keeper on the road to all promotions out of his school, disagreed. As a result, Bob became still another of Jack's enemies.

Members of this clique were also persons of no small talent. They had to be. For Jack and his cronies were always sniping at them in return. Meanwhile Jack and his supporters tried to provide as few openings for criticism as possible. As this study drew to a close, the principal's clique was still in control. For in public school life, as in most other areas, the prizes are often defended by some pretty tough people. You seldom take anything away from them easily.

A few Pleasant Avenue teachers belonged to a district-wide clique. All the members came to the district at approximately the same time–following World War II. All were about the same age. Some were administrators. Some not. All were very ambitious. And, most important, all shared the belief that, being the original academic settlers in this area, they therefore enjoyed certain squatters' rights. All promotions, they said, should go to them.

The leader of this group was Tom Osborn, a talented high school principal. Short, fat, and pugnacious, he worked very hard and knew a lot about how to run a school. Unlike the typical poor-spirited drudge, who works out his life in a classroom for around $5,000 a year and expects no more, this man had plans to make schoolteaching really pay off for a change. Since his salary was already $19,000, he was well on his way.

Many people, thinking all teachers are pitifully underpaid, scarcely realize that such men exist. Yet most school districts of any size have several men on the payroll who make more than successful businessmen. Indeed, the parent who hears his son say that he wants to go into schoolteaching should be delighted. For if the son goes into administration, he may end up making $25,000 or $30,000 a year. And this even in some pretty small districts.

Naturally, such a talented man attracts followers. In Tom's case, these formed a bowling team. Once a week, after a game or two, they went to a tavern. There the conversation frequently dwelled on the good things of this world.

If he ever got the superintendent's job, Tom would say, he would be in a position to help some of the good teachers here who were his friends. He had it all planned. Jack, for example, would get the business manager's position. Flaherty (over there behind the potato chips) would get the high school principalship he would leave open. Ryan would be principal of the new junior high. In other words, everyone would get something. It would be a veritable feast–if only we could get rid of the present superintendent.

Even teachers not members of this clique thought it a good policy to keep on the right side of Tom Osborn. Because everyone in the district was absolutely confident that he and his clique would finally seize power. And when they did, it would be convenient to have friends up at headquarters.

However (and here comes an important point), the members of the Board of Education kept interfering with Tom's plans. To his great disappointment, they kept giving the superintendent's job to people from outside the district. Someone said the board was not going to let one clique gain complete control–in which case the members might go to sleep on the job. Instead, it played one clique against another, thus stimulating all teachers to do their best.

This so infuriated Tom and his close associates that they decided to control the district by controlling the school board in the first place. Jack passed down the names of board members Tom considered worthy of reelection. He also provided the names of those whom Tom had marked for political death. We were supposed to tell our friends in the community to vote accordingly.

Strange to relate, membership in this group also signalized teaching quality. Remember that all members were hardworking and insanely ambitious men. Such men are seldom mediocrities or incompetents: This was a combat outfit bent on throwing out school board members and capturing $20,000-a-year positions. They could not afford to have a nut in their midst.

The last group of any importance in our lives was the one gathered around the superintendent, the headquarters group. Each new superintendent brought in with him a whole new crew of assistant superintendents and other administrators. For the custom was that when any superintendent fell from power, he dragged down with him all his supporters. The new superintendent, therefore, had the opportunity to appoint people he knew he could work with and trust. It is the same in most political set-ups. These became his clique, closely knit and loyal.

What these clique members had in common was each owed his job to the superintendent—and also each was an extremely talented individual. For you do not get this high up in the administrative hierarchy unless you are an intelligent and hard-working person.

You would think that so much ability in one group would result in a clique so powerful as to be absolutely unbeatable. This is true in some districts. There, not only the assistant superintendents, but also the building principals, owe their jobs to the superintendent. If any teacher in one of the schools says a disloyal word about the superintendent, the principal gets rid of him immediately. In return the superintendent will do anything under the sun for the principal. The principal has only to pick up his phone.

This system is unbeatable and probably owes much to its founder, Adolf Hitler. For it produces an absolutely frictionless and quiet-running school. This, we said, is what the public wants. The average taxpayer thinks that if all is peace and quiet up at the school, then much valuable learning must be going on.

However, in our district no superintendent ever lasted more than three or four years. Therefore, just as one began to build a little clique of loyal supporters, he left and his clique either left or fell apart.

I must admit, therefore, that at Pleasant Avenue School that elusive person the good teacher, far from being a pious person who stood aloof from all office politics, was instead just a likely to be someone who played office politics like mad.

13

We lived in a time of transition. (Who doesn't?) One world was just coming into being, and another passing out. In the prosperity that followed World War II, common laborers suddenly began to make more than teachers of long experience and education. Grade school teachers began to make more than many university professors. Principals made more than anyone else, including many doctors and lawyers.

Then, too, a great population explosion created a serious shortage of teachers. To top it all off, teachers all over the country suddenly became more aggressive in their demands for higher salaries. They began winning substantial increases just about everywhere. For public school teachers, it seemed the good old days were right now.

Naturally this had to have repercussions in our little school. Some of the younger teachers began to agitate for higher salaries. They formed the teachers' salary committee for the purpose of negotiating with the school board.

This caused the teachers to choose up sides for still another debate. (Apparently everything in education is debatable.) Those on one side said a good teacher would naturally expect a good salary. That is how you could tell he was good. Realizing that he had talent, he would naturally put a high price on himself. A mediocrity, on the other hand, would never dare ask for more money. He would feel himself lucky to have any job at all, at any wage.

Holders of this opinion were for the most part young married men. All had beautiful wives, always pregnant, and large families. In our time, large families were in fashion. It was nothing to find a teacher with ten children. One, by mistake, had been practicing the rhythm system out of rhythm. It took money to support such families.

Higher salaries, these men said, would mean higher quality people coming into the profession. "If you paid teachers $20,000," one man said, "then some of the best college students would leave medical and dental school and go into teaching. Can you imagine a high I.Q. college student killing himself studying nights and weekends so that some day he can land a big $4,000-a-year teaching job?"

There was also a feeling that teachers were slowly losing prestige, that the public did not respect teachers as much as it used to. Less and less was there any great prestige in simply being a college man. Everyone and his neighbor now attended some college somewhere. All of a sudden the day was all through when anything a teacher said in the classroom the parents immediately backed up in the home. (The beating the child received at school would be nothing compared to the one he got at home.) "Nowadays," one woman said, "when a teacher tells a child to do something, many a parent either calls up or comes to the school and argues." "A teacher used to get paid partly in public respect," one young man said, "But now if he does not take his pay home in the form of money, he may not take it home at all."

"No! No! No! And no!" shouted the teachers with the opposite opinion. "The good teacher works, not for money, but for love of the work. If you pay teachers more, this will attract into the profession people interested only in money—and so not dedicated."

Holders of this opinion were for the most part elderly married ladies. These privately admitted that they used their paychecks mainly for pin money or to pay for something special, such as a new home or a child's college education.

One day after school a group of teachers were looking out the window at the beautiful trees and shrubs that grew near the school, and discussing the wonderful raise the board had given us. Some with master's degrees and considerable experience were actually going to make $10,000-a-year. This was more than many of us had ever dreamed of making, no matter what occupation we went into.

Anyway, on this particular day a sweet little old lady over in the corner suddenly shouted over to ask what everyone was talking about.

"The raise!" someone shouted in return. "You know, the raise!"

The dear old soul replied that she did not know we had received a raise. Besides, she added, she never had any more to do with mere money than she had to. Wages and hours were the preoccupations of clerks and ditchdiggers—not professionals.

An elderly lady once stood up at a faculty meeting and said that she was proud that she had worked most of her life for approximately $3,000-a-year. Then she sat down. By this statement she thought she had proved her quality. Younger teachers turned around and stared at her in amazement. They could hardly understand what she was talking about. $3,000. Who could live decently on that?

Every year, some older teachers went to our superintendent and told him that they were not in sympathy with those young men on the teachers' salary committee who were always asking for higher wages. One even went to the extreme of saying that she wanted her salary cut. "I'm not worth what I'm getting now," she said.

These dear old souls nearly drove the younger teachers crazy. In fact, the younger teachers wanted to take them out behind the school and strangle them, to shut them up. By such statements these oldsters thought that they ingratiated themselves with the superintendent. What they did not realize was that the superintendent worked harder than anyone else to raise salaries. He was sick of people stopping him on the street and complaining about the low quality of the teachers. He wanted a greater choice.

"You see those old ladies there?" he once said to a group

of us. He pointed to a group of old ladies who always sat by themselves. "They're what hold this profession back. If you paid them $100 a month, they'd think it just fine. Somehow, they'd manage to get along."

The surprising thing about these ladies was not that they should hold an opinion contrary to that of the majority, but the fervor with which they fought against theirs and everybody else's raises. One very pugnacious old lady, for example, once held off all the men on the faculty. Surprisingly, she advanced some very good arguments. "If you get the raise," she yelled, "will you work any faster? No? Any longer hours? Will you be any smarter? No? Then why should you get more money? Answer me that, young man!"

Younger teachers kept asking why these elderly ladies opposed raises. Someone suggested that they might have a very low opinion of themselves. Maybe years of low pay and low prestige had convinced these women that they were pretty worthless creatures. But younger teachers, not having gone through such belittling experiences, had a higher opinion of themselves. Then again, maybe they were right. Maybe they were not worth more.

Many townspeople joined in the argument. For years they had been screaming for quality teachers. Now that they had them, they were stupified to find that such people wanted money. They never dreamed that a quality teacher would expect a quality salary.

In connection with salaries, one might ask how the economic class from which teachers come affects teaching efficiency. Our teachers, like most others, belonged to the lower part of the middle class. We worshipped all the middle class virtues. Most of us lived by and expected every other teacher to live by principles of hard work, thrift, saving, sobriety, honesty, self-sufficiency, and civic responsibility.

Therefore, those teachers who said they were saving to buy their own homes and doing nothing more exciting on week-ends than mowing their lawns we called good teachers. The few, however, who spent too much for clothes or took too many trips to Sun Valley we censured.

But not every one of our teachers came from the middle class. Every year, it seemed, we received one new teacher from the upper middle class. This was usually the daughter of a very successful surgeon or business man who for idealistic reasons wanted to teach. Within a year or two, each realized her mistake and went back to her own social set.

All were made to feel most welcome in our midst. For all were good-looking, respectful, and extremely hard workers. Apparently Radcliffe and Vassar get their students used to plenty of hard work.

One young lady lived with her parents in a 19 room house, with bathrooms having solid gold fixtures. She drove a Jaguar. She even knew Dina Merrill. Yet they say that every evening she corrected papers far into the night as though her life depended on it.

How many teachers came to us from the lower class would be hard to tell. Most of our teachers did not want to talk about their economic backgrounds. However, judging from informal conversations over six years, I would judge that quite a few of us were the sons or daughters of window cleaners, sewing machine salesmen, barbers, and taxi drivers.

After all, public school teaching has for years been world-famous as a way for the talented son of a poor family to pull himself up in life, to arrive at a better social level than that of his parents. Though he might have tremendous ability, he might never be able to go to a medical school or law school at the other end of the state. But somehow his parents can afford to finance four years at the local normal school. In this manner, the poorer classes have for years furnished the public schools with talented men and women–many with enough ability to be much more than public school teachers.

I think I will have to give myself as an example of a teacher who came up from the lower class. My parents were on relief so long that one day when my mother asked what I wanted to be when I grew up, I automatically replied a relief case like father. I could not imagine any other kind of life. My mother once remarked that when we went on W.P.A. we actually began to eat better food.

But in high school I was a good student, and to my complete amazement, I won a college scholarship. My high school teachers (God bless them) all urged me to go on to college. (Can you wonder today why I worship such people?) But my poor father! Looking back on it all now, I can only guess at the anguish it must have caused him trying to keep in good at the relief office, and at the same time, keep a son in college. Maybe some kindly social worker looked the other way.

Now the question comes up, how good did our teachers think we upward-mobile people were? The best teachers in the world, our teachers said. Indeed, there was some feeling that teachers such as I might enjoy special powers in a lower middle class community such as Pleasant Valley, California. We felt that we understood the children and the parents better.

One of our Latin American teachers spoke Spanish with parents, which delighted both parents and children. Our one Negro teacher, we thought, served as a good example of what a Negro child might become. Looking at her, any Negro boy or girl could see the excellent person he or she might someday be. Indeed, I had hopes that even my example might inspire a few.

So it seemed that you could not tell much about a teacher's quality from the social class from which he came. Well then, how could you tell a good teacher?

14

One year our superintendent suddenly announced that from now on we were going to have something called ability grouping. Every child in the school would have to take an intelligence test. Then all the talented first graders would go into one room—and work there at their own speed. The average first graders would go into another room—and work at theirs. And all the slow learners would while away their time in yet a third room. The other grades would be grouped in the same way.

This plan did seem to help the children. However, there were also some odd side effects. For example, some average quality teachers when they got a talented class, suddenly began to look brilliant. At long last there were no discipline problems. The class practically ran itself. For one characteristic of the talented pupil is that so often he is self-disciplined, industrious, and polite.

One talented class did the work in the textbooks so rapidly that the teacher decided to devote the rest of the year to interesting projects—a school newspaper, a play, French lessons, fascinating exhibits for the display case in the front hall. Since the room was so packed with talent, all he had to do was give the most general of suggestions (such as "Why don't we have a class newspaper?")—and the pupils would do everything perfectly. Parents and others commented that this man was working miracles. And he was.

The poor man who received the lowest I.Q. group, however, found himself doing everything wrong. First, there was the discipline problem. He soon learned that when you put thirty or so unacademically inclined in one room, discipline problems multiply astronomically. For the low I.Q. pupil is very often convinced that he has a gift for humor and public entertainment. What else does he have to offer? If he would keep quiet, then no one would ever discover that he was retarded. But no! He feels that he must regale the rest of the pupils with his jokes and antics.

When you looked at one of these classes, you got a shock. Everyone sat there grinning wildly or laughing hysterically. The teacher would be lecturing on some boring subject, such as the parts of a sentence, and the pupils would nearly fall out of their seats laughing.

Furthermore, such children were always doing something that got on the teachers' nerves. For, far from feeling inferior, these children often delighted in torturing their teachers.

"Holy smoke!" a boy shouted one day. "The people in this *National Geographic* magazine have no clothes on! Look at the woman. Tee hee."

"Richard," the teacher shouted in return, "if I have to tell you once more to shut that mouth of yours . . . Give me that magazine!"

"What did I do? What did I do? Name one thing! Name one thing!"

And so on and on. All the poor teacher did all day was argue with the students.

Teachers had to work hard to get any kind of results out of these. One's method was to trick his pupils into learning. If, for example, he wanted them to go to the library, then he did not even mention the word library. For another characteristic of the unacademically inclined is no matter what you mention, he does not want to do it. Instead this teacher talked somewhat as follows.

"Oh, look what I found here–45 interesting mathematical problems. What fun doing them! When shall we start?"

"Never," the classmembers would shout.

"But wait," he would add. "We have a conflict here. We are also supposed to go to the library today. Only if we go to the library then we will not be able to do the 45 problems. Which shall we do?"

"The library," everyone would shout.

One day a teacher told of a darling, goldenhaired little girl–with an I.Q. of 60–who brought a plant to school growing in a bowl of Quaker Oats. She placed it in the window so it would catch the sun. At snack time, a little boy poured his milk on it and ate it–plant and all. This caused the little girl to stand up and slug it out with the little boy. And, of course, the teacher had to pull these two apart.

We soon discovered that only a very few teachers could handle the slow learners. Many a promising young man or woman tried, but after a year or two transferred to other districts in which there was no ability grouping.

I can recall only one teacher who was widely believed to be doing a good job of teaching a low (intelligence) class. This energetic and tough woman quickly transformed all her little jokers and funmakers into quiet little behavers. When she marched them down the hall in two perfect lines, they were all so well behaved that you would swear this was a talented class. "With a good teacher," one excellent man once said, "even a low class looks good. With a mediocre teacher, however, even a high class might look low."

But this woman was an exceptionally talented person. Usually it was very difficult to find people who could handle the retarded. At one time, the shortage became so great that the best teachers held down the slow learners, and the mediocre taught the talented. What an about face.

This shortage, therefore, called into existence a new definition of a good teacher–a tough (and not necessarily intelligent or sensitive) person who could handle the slow learners. One such teacher maintained that his own stupidity made him a better teacher. He said that, because he knew how slow learners thought and felt, he could understand and reach such pupils better than anyone else in the building. He criticized one very intelligent young man. This man, he said, was not a good teacher because he always talked over the heads of his students.

It did seem that the first teacher had special powers with the retarded. After a few weeks with him, these oversized, and often insolent, sixth graders turned into quiet and occasionally industrious students. He could get work out of pupils whom other teachers had considered absolutely hopeless. With his love of authority out in front working for him and his lack of intelligence scarcely showing, he made a very satisfactory career for himself.

His method of teaching was simply to take it easy on the kids. He took them outside and played ball with them a lot. The children seemed to sense that he too did not have much use for learning. Therefore, without making too many demands on each other, the two managed to pass the time. The principal, pitifully grateful to have this problem off his hands, did not ask questions.

As I said before, this was a time of terrific population explosion. Every day, it seemed the principal brought some new pupil to some poor, overworked teacher's room. Then he and the teacher tried to figure out where they could fit one more desk into this already overcrowded room.

"How about in front of the sink over there?"

"Yes, but then no one could ever get to the thing."

"Well, that's about the only way it can be done. Ha. Ha. No plan is perfect, I guess."

As nearly every classroom filled up with 35, 40, and even more, it became apparent that some teachers were very good at handling large numbers of children. They did not care how many children were in their rooms. Apparently there was no limit to the numbers these people could teach.

Then something else became apparent. It developed that those who could adequately teach such large numbers were extremely rare. In our school there were only two or three such master teachers. The rest were lucky if they could instruct 25. For every pupil over that number, the service had to be watered down.

This called into existence still another definition of a good teacher–one who could handle kids in quantity. Never mind how intelligent he happened to be. How many could he handle was the question.

Jack also had a way of handing out room assignments and equipment that told something about your quality or at least about your standing in the school. For example, he always put his best teachers in rooms facing the street and near the office. In that way, visitors, who might look in a window or door, would never see what they should not see. All hopelessly inept teachers had rooms way in the back of the building. When a visitor asked to see a class, the principal always took him to just one or two classes, run by very superior teachers. These were the showplaces. The visitor never saw some classrooms. If he did, he might never again pay his school taxes.

Even the presence of the most common office supplies said something about your standing. The principal, who would buy anything under the sun to keep a good teacher happy, would not give anything to a mediocrity. One day, I asked the principal's secretary for some stencils. "Are you in the group that makes good use of stencils?" she asked. "I'm only supposed to give them to those who know how to use them. The rest mess up too many. Waste of money."

Jack made all such assignments after talking with the more powerful teachers (in order not to set off a revolution). Therefore, when you saw someone with a good room and loads of equipment, the chances were that you saw at the same time what the majority called a good teacher (though naturally some paid no attention to this teacher-judging business).

15

Year after year parents complained like crazy about the schools. You could hardly blame them. Many were paying as high as a hundred dollars a month in school taxes on the plainest of houses. To add to the fun, the Catholic Church opened a beautiful school in a nearby town and proceeded to do a perfectly good job, while not charging the taxpayers a cent. Several teachers, and even some administrators, sent their children there. None, however, had ever sent a child to Pleasant Avenue School. One explained that he would not dare to expose his son to the kind of education dished out here. Parents knew this and were understandable resentful.

So much criticism from the outside created a need for a quiet, frictionless machine on the inside–one not needing any investigation. We did not need internal debate and self-criticism of the kind glorified at the university. Our administrators often explained that we absolutely must not stir up the voters. Budgets were difficult enough to pass. Some just squeaked through. Every vote counted.

Have you noticed what quiet, obsequious, burned-out, spiritless and ingratiating people teachers often are? One Pleasant Valley lady who was a widow thought all our men teachers had lost their masculinity. "Show me a real man around here," she said. "I don't see any. Where are they?"

One possible reason for this lack of strong, forceful personalities at Pleasant Avenue might have been the great need for all teachers to stay out of trouble with the locals. Many teachers' idea of a good teacher, therefore, was a passive-dependent person. He never acted. He reacted. He never initiated action. Instead, he waited for things to happen to him.

He never revealed his personal feelings on any subject. He avoided standing for anything or being personally conspicuous. He went along. He played it safe. In a way he was like a wild animal who had once been wounded and had developed the ability to smell trouble while it was still a long way off.

For this teaching life, though rewarding, is sometimes dangerous. Any Pleasant Valley citizen, by simply picking up the phone and calling the superintendent, could get a teacher into all kinds of trouble. And the citizens knew it. Even if the teacher proved that he had been in the right, he was still all wrong.

One evening one of the teachers chaperoned a group of pupils to a basketball game. While there, he asked a drunk in the stands to stop swearing. Besides, the drunk was sitting in a section reserved for students. This man immediately started to fight. Would you believe it, the next day he not only sued the teacher but also the school district? The superintendent, not overjoyed to find himself in the middle of a $100,000 lawsuit, began to think how nice life would be with that teacher out of the district. All he brought was trouble.

One day, a woman wearing shorts and high heels came into the school. All the little 12 year old boys started whistling not realizing in their innocence that she was simply an old bag. Seeing this rumpus, a teacher asked her to leave.

You guessed it. She went to the nearest phone booth and called the superintendent. Not being able to see over the telephone how she was dressed, he sympathized with her. "Why, visitors are always welcome," he said. He would certainly call the principal of that building and extract an apology right away.

The principal, passing this good news on to the teacher,

remarked that this woman must have all kinds of political pull; for the superintendent was really boiling.

"But who," the teacher asked, "in their wildest imagination would have guessed that a woman wearing shorts in the middle of the day in a public school would have political pull?"

"A good teacher," the principal replied. "That's who."

The young teacher who wrote to the great corporation to complain about their product, expected that he would receive a letter from the company president thanking him for pointing out the defect. Instead, he received a phone call from his superintendent telling him to shut up. An important local was the agent for that company. The great company then went happily on manufacturing and selling educational junk.

One day, a teacher asked humorously if I had yet found "The Good Teacher." I replied that I had not.

Well, he had, he said and led the way down the hall. He pointed in the door of a certain classroom. There she was! Miss Virginia Phibbs was the oldest, best liked, and most anonymous member of the staff. She stayed to herself so much that she even ate lunch in her own classroom. No one had ever been inside her house. In fact, few even knew where she lived. And she had taught in the district for a lifetime.

All the other older teachers also made a passion of anonymity. That way, one explained, when the members of this or that community group attacked the schools, they could not possible name them. How could they? These locals would not know that such quiet teachers were even on the payroll.

It is significant that only one out of 98 past and present teachers ever lived in Pleasant Valley. The reason was not that Pleasant Valley was anything other than a wonderful place to raise kids and grow old in. The reason, one teacher explained, was that if you lived in Pleasant Valley, townspeople would learn your personal, political, and religious opinions. And though most of them were lovely people, a few would become your enemies.

You went to a meeting of the Democratic Party and now your neighbor wants you fired. You stayed home from school Monday and your landlady strongly suspects that you were not sick at all. Her brother is a good friend of the superintendent. Rather than put up with much of this, the Pleasant Avenue teacher lived as far away as possible.

Recently, a teacher called to my attention that, though the superintendent was easily the most important member of our staff, still not one of us knew whether he was a Democrat or Republican, Catholic or Protestant, or anything else about him. I could not help thinking that the old man had not lasted, lo, these many years in the school business by shooting his mouth off all the time. He was shrewd enough to provide his critics with the smallest opening through which to attack him.

The good teacher was even careful of what he said and did in front of the little children. For they controlled their parents, and the parents controlled the school board, and the school board controlled the teachers. It was a vicious circle. This teacher made it his business to learn which children had parents who are very decent people—and which had parents who are dangerously deranged or politically powerful. In this way he knew when to crack down on a kid—and when to look the other way.

"That remark you made in front of the students," one man told another, "both you and I know was just a little harmless humor; yet it will be repeated at many a dinner table tonight." He was right. Ninety-nine per cent of the trouble at Pleasant Avenue was caused by a big mouth. You absolutely could not be too careful. Keep your mouth shut was the best policy.

Unfortunately, I think such super-carefulness produced some of the mediocrity and bureaucratic time-serving for which public schools are famous. Younger teachers, observing that the less they did, the less trouble they got into, soon took up the habit of doing very little. Youthful zeal got replaced by buck-passing and goofing-off.

Teachers told how, when they first started, they pitched

in and worked hard. They kept kids after school and gave them individual lessons. They took classes on trips. They joined the American Legion and the local church. It was not long, however, before they found to their amazement that such actions only got them in trouble. Now they lived far away. And their main interest was in closing time and their hobbies at home. Who can blame them?

The public notion of the good teacher as the inherently and necessarily free man is sometimes wrong. A university may be a group of autonomous individuals held together only by a common devotion to the central heating system, but a public school faculty is often a group of hired hands who do as they are told.

This system exerts continual pressure on the individual to be disciplined, conforming, and unquestioning. The good teacher ends up a kind of impersonal medium. The superintendent dreams up policy–after carefully consulting the more powerful members of the school board. He hands this to the principal. The principal then calls one more boring faculty meeting. After laughing gently, he announces that here on these mimeographed sheets are the latest orders from headquarters.

"Oh, my God!" someone would exclaim at a typical Pleasant Avenue faculty meeting. "more regulations!"

Then, after everyone had read in silence for a while, another teacher would say, "Jack, it says here we must henceforth apply for emergency leave ten days in advance. Suppose my relatives don't tell me ten days before they are going to die? These old people can't always set the date, you know. What then?" A snicker would follow around the room.

After waiting for the room to quiet down, Jack would explain very slowly that these latest regulations were the superintendent's idea, not his. "As a matter of fact," he would say, "I don't understand some of them, myself."

Yet this requirement that we all do the same thing in the same way, like many another in public school life, had good reason for its existence. It must be borne in mind that a public school is a mass production operation and requires much coordination. Thus, unless the third grade teacher teaches short division, then the fourth grade teacher will not be able to build long division on it. Again, unless the fifth grade teacher grades the same way as the fourth grade teacher, then some parent might scream, "How come Junior was an A student last year, but a C student this one? What's wrong?" A teacher with strong opinions on educational processes might, therefore, be a hopeles misfit.

Indeed, so much did a good teacher live strictly within regulations that one commented that, not only were his thoughts controlled by the system, but also his bowels. He said, that since he got his free period at exactly the same time each day, he had developed the habit of going to the toilet right on schedule.

Another teacher commented facetiously that in the district in the South where he used to work, where they required all teachers to attend church, even the teachers' place in the next world was controlled by the system. Previous to joining that district, this teacher had done everything to lose his immortal soul. But, since this district had forced him to go to church regularly, he and every other teacher had qualified for a heavenly crown.

Of course, so much surrender of independent judgment, so much conformity, had to have an effect on the teachers. I think it produced much routine opinion, much apathy, and in the end much mediocrity. Perhaps this partly explains why public school teachers write few books on education, contribute few articles to their own journals, and make almost no speeches to learned societies. These are all done for them by college professors, who never go near public schools.

I suggest, therefore, that the next time someone objects to the education his child receives, perhaps he should not automatically blame the teacher. If he investigates a little, he might discover that this teacher is not a hopeless bungler who does not care how he works. Instead, he might find that this teacher is a very intelligent and dedicated person—who is simply taking orders. He has to. He might even find that this teacher does not like the way things are run, either, any more than anyone else does.

Another opinion of Pleasant Avenue teachers on the subject of teacher quality was that a good teacher would be able to get along with most other teachers. Intellectual piece-work, by its very nature requires an operator who works smoothly with others. It is not necessary that this benchworker be wildly popular all over the plant, but it is absolutely necessary that he not work against the other men.

Therefore, in order to keep to an absolute minimum the number of enemies, the good teacher would go to almost any extreme. In public, he would fall all over his worst enemy, pretending he was a friend. If you told him that you heard he did not like the teacher across the hall, then in order to kill this rumor, he would invite this teacher to his home to dinner. I asked one experienced woman what she would do if she saw someone stealing something, such as a typewriter, from the school. "Say nothing," she replied. "Might make an enemy that way."

Shortly afterward, a teacher walked out the back door with a record player. When I told the principal, he was disgusted to be presented with this emergency. He simply said that he was taking "due note" of the fact, and it would be taken care of soon. That was the last anyone heard of the matter. I could not help thinking that maybe Jack also had risen to his present position because he offended very few people.

In fact, teachers who really flourished–who got promoted–were the ones who were extremely popular, uncritical of others, and had absolutely no enemies. We all knew two very excellent men in another school who would never amount to anything, talent or no talent. Years ago they had made the wrong enemies up at headquarters. Now every time someone mentioned their good work up there, these would be sure to say something against them.

Still another way you could tell a good teacher, I heard teachers say, was by his ability to keep his mouth shut–more specifically his ability to tell the parents absolutely nothing.

I remember when we first installed ability grouping, we faced the possibility to having to tell some parents that their children were dull and so must sit in a classroom with other dull children–some of whom are decidedly unattractive. A father told that the schools are preparing his son for a lifetime as a filling station attendant can be difficult to control.

To solve this one, our principal suggested that we never tell the parents what kind of a class their children were in. "If one asks you," he said, "simply tell him that the child is in one of the nicest classes in the school. Such a statement, while telling a parent absolutely nothing, still has a calming effect on the lay mind." Strange to relate, Jack was absolutely right.

One day the mother of one of the children volunteered to work for nothing, helping our energetic music teacher, who was putting on, of all things, *Oklahoma*. The principal turned her down cold. "Can you imagine," he asked me, "what would happen if she saw what goes on across the hall from the music room?"

When I looked in the door of that room, I had to admit he was right again. It was recess period and because it was raining outside, the children had to stay inside. So the children were amusing themselves. As usual, the little girls were all perfectly behaved. But the boys! One was trying to escape through the window. Another was playfully strangling his little companion. "You don't like this world," he shouted. "Try the next!"

Every once in a while, our school secretary broadcast over the intercom: "The clocks are running slow. Pay no attention to the clocks." This was code understood only by teachers; it meant strangers in the building.

In our time, for some odd reason, many community members were violently opposed to the ideas of John Dewey. Yet every one of our teachers admired him. We could see that if a child does not experience, then all he might learn would be a mess of meaningless words. One little boy once showed me a theme he was writing. "The chief exports of the State of Pennsylvania," he wrote, "are coal, iron, and the Bureau of

Mines." He told me privately that he had no idea what he was writing.

But we did not dare tell the members of the public the way we felt. Publicly, therefore, we professed great shock at progressive education. "Oh, yes," one teacher said, "just the three R's. That's all we want in the classroom. Nothing more. Nothing revolutionary."

The principal always censored all outgoing mail. "You didn't stick to the party line," he once said to me, winking. And he handed back something I had written. Sure enough, I had deviated. I had said that our teachers were not perfect, that we made mistakes, the same as anyone else. "That," Jack said, "might provide an opening for critics. That's the way we talk among ourselves. But don't forget that there's a difference between the way we talk among ourselves and the way we talk to the members of the public."

In fact, so close was this censorship that it even extended to the school board. According to our code, no teacher could ever communicate with a board member. If a teacher had something to say to one, he had to first tell it to the principal. The principal would tell the superintendent. And the superintendent then told the member of the board. One of these excellent men once told me that the amount of information that finally worked its way up through this filtration system was extremely small.

At this point someone might ask what was to stop any teacher from subtly leaking out bits of gossip. This could be very risky. For, as the superintendent once warned, "If a story gets out, we can always ask townspeople where they got their information."

This system of censorship worked very well. Few stories uncomplimentary to the school ever got past the front door. One time two boys set fire to the building and did several thousands of dollars worth of damage. About a week later, while talking to a local lady reputed to be the town blabbermouth who knew everything, I carelessly mentioned the fire. "What fire?" she asked.

16

We had another interesting teacher, Paul Lombardi. A quiet, withdrawn fellow in his early 30's, Paul had been a fighter pilot on the aircraft carrier, *Enterprise,* in one of our country's numerous wars. I would have sworn that anyone with such a distinguished war record would surely get some extra respect. But no. Paul had no better reputation than another teacher who had not even been drafted.

In fact, this second man received even more respect. For he possessed an Irish wit and a friendly personality that both teachers and students found most attractive. There was always a group of students, and even teachers, following him around to listen to his latest quips. With this personality alone, many of us said, he must have great power to do good among the students.

I heard more than one teacher say that any teacher's personality was one of his most important professional tools. With it, they said, he either attracted pupils to whatever he was teaching–or he repelled them. They believed that when a child says he likes school, very often what he means is that he likes his teacher.

In the make-up of that personality, intelligence assumed great importance. Perhaps because knowledge is any teacher's stock-in-trade, all the teachers I talked to or observed looked for that first. For example, they expected teachers to show a rather profound knowledge of teaching techniques and child psychology. Thus, the man who said that all little Howard McCollum needed was love, made the remark in front of three of Howard's former teachers. These had had a long and fairly painful association with him. And all proceeded to jump all over this man. They explained that what Howard needed was not love, but a good kick in the pants instead. Love indeed!

We required, furthermore, than any teacher display a considerable fund of miscellaneous information. Remember that an elementary school teacher teaches all the subjects. He cannot, therefore, act like the university professor who delights to tell you that he is totally ignorant of every subject outside his specialty.

After years of teaching all subjects, a good elementary school teacher's mind is supposed to end up a veritable treasury of information. Why was King Arthur's Round Table round? Why did Bleeding Kansas bleed? What is a griffin? A good teacher, we said, would know. Or at least know where to quickly find out. Stupidity, our teachers believed, was the one sin never forgiven.

I often heard teachers say (and no one objected) that any teacher also has to be in excellent physical health. The world of the blackboard jungle requires nothing less. I even heard a few teachers say that they went to bed every night at eight o'clock–all worn out. Some of the ladies spent all of their long, beautiful vacations just resting.

I remember one afternoon we were all outside loading the children onto the buses. Even though this was not the last day of the school year, the children all waved wildly as if they would never see us again. Suddenly, a boy dashed out of line and between two buses–which is plainly dangerous and against all regulations. I shouted, "Stop, you fool!" which I thought was all anyone could expect of me.

But one outstanding man in his early 40's took off after the boy. This boy, a sixth grader and a fast runner, knew the teacher was after him and he ran way to the other end of the playground. This excellent teacher finally caught him. (The boy explained that he thought he saw someone he knew over there, and he wished to talk with this person.)

The teacher marched the boy to the office and informed the principal (who was not too interested). Then he phoned the mother (who also was not overly delighted to be disturbed). Finally, after giving the boy a lecture on safety, he had to give him a ride home in his car. For by this time all the buses had left. And this is just a sample of the energetic way this man worked every day. You had to work this vigorously to do the job properly. If you did less, you would never impress our teachers.

Next, consider the problem of standing all day in front of a roomful of youngsters at an age when they catch every cold, virus, and every other disease going around. In almost any season one of them would be sure to have something–and be coughing away. Why, some teachers even came down with the same childhood diseases the children had–including the mumps. One had to be a pretty good man to survive that.

Perhaps you have heard that mental illness is the disease of the school-teacher. The nutty, absent-minded professor is a fairly well-known type. But this is not true. No occupational group has more mental illness than any other. Ulcers and heart trouble happen to be the diseases of school-teachers.

Our teachers believed that any good teacher should be in reasonably good mental health. Mere acting would not do here. The nutty professor might be beloved on the outside, but he would never be accepted by fellow teachers.

A teacher's personality, I heard several say, is always out there for the pupils to observe and imitate. Children learn more from their teachers than the famous three R's. They also learn some of their teachers' attitudes, manners, habits, and values.

In fact, our teachers said that sometimes the main benefit in studying with certain teachers is the student gets to contact, and perhaps come under the influence of some wholesome personality. Take Mrs. Berenberg, for example, a very beautiful and refined lady, the wife of a struggling young attorney. When you talked to her, you could not help thinking of all the training her parents had built into her. I hear several people remark that somehow her pupils would take on some of her superior manners, gentility, and ideals.

Only two of our teachers were considered by others to be eccentric. Too much tension, or something else, had damaged the nerves of one so that when she talked, she stuttered. She occasionally talked to herself. Though a couple of the teachers (me for one) genuinely liked her, the majority shunned her.

The other, when he gave the lesson on the frog, used to get up on his desk, then crouch down, and jump off. When he gave some other lesson, he did something else just as looney. His pupils were always in hysterics. He surely put on a good show.

"You're making your kids nuts like you," one of the men teachers once said to him. This man might have been right. It did seem that pupils who had been known by former teachers to be self-controlled and respectful workers, after listening to and watching this teacher for a year, all turned into little jokers and eccentrics just like him. Even though the teachers also nearly died laughing at his antics, when they got through laughing they did not vote him a very good teacher.

No doubt you have heard that teaching requires strong nerves. And you are so right. There was much agreement among us that any good teacher would have a particularly strong set. As strong as those of a statue in the park would be about right. Every class has its problem pupils who wore down the nerves of the poor teacher. I would say three of these jewels to each classroom would be about average.

"So I shook this kid good, see?" explained one man, "and bawled the hell out of him. Then I noticed that all the while he was smiling. And I remembered that the last time I bawled him out, he smiled then too. It suddenly occurred to me that this kid *likes* punishment. Now I don't know what to do with him. Thank God it's Friday."

I have known teachers who had been struck by a pupil, cursed by a parent, and falsely accused by the principal, joke about the whole thing. "Win a few. Lose a few," said one such teacher, pouring himself a cup of our lousy coffee. You had to be able to shake off your troubles like that quite often. Otherwise you would never earn the reputation of a good teacher at Pleasant Avenue.

Good looks did not count much with us though. The plainest and sometimes the ugliest of people enjoyed great respect and popularity. The most respected woman on our staff, for example, was fat, had heavy Indian-like features, and walked like a wrestler. When she strode down the hall, her arms swung back and forth, and did not even touch her body.

You could easily imagine that early in her life she must have realized, perhaps after some cruel experiences, that she could never get by in this world on her looks. She would either have to be good at her work, or she would have no work at all.

And good she was. While other teachers took their ease in the lounge, Irene worked on and on in her classroom. Naturally all of this work had to produce some results. So, when visitors asked who was that definitely unlovely lady over there, the reply was, "The best teacher in the school."

Another teacher was a handsome and affable fellow of about 30. Probably realizing that he had good looks, he improved on them. He exercised every day, so that he looked fit–instead of flaccid and paunchy like the rest of us. He wore the most conservative of clothes–which alone guaranteed that he would be well-dressed.

Unfortunately he had no interest in school-teaching. Bill used to walk up to another teacher and say, "Hey, man, watch my class while I fuck off." This statement sounded so shocking that you naturally assumed he must be kidding. He wasn't. He loafed most of the day away.

Still as Bill walked down the hall with one hand in his pocket, pausing now and then to say a word of greeting to all he passed, for he had plenty of time for conversation, he looked so distinguished that visitors knew instinctively that he must surely be the most prominent teacher in the school.

He was not. He had the reputation of the worst teacher in the building.

While on the subject of personality, it is interesting to consider the age-old question of whether married or unmarried people make the best teachers. As late as one generation ago, people believed that unmarried women made the best teachers. Public schools in those days were referred to facetiously as Protestant Nunneries. The love which would have gone to a husband and children was supposed to go instead to the school-children. The time which would have gone to cooking and cleaning for a husband and family was presumed to go to the preparation of lessons and the perusal of learned journals.

But the great shortage of teachers following World War II forced the school board to hire many married ladies. All these worked out fine. The woman with a husband and three children to cook and clean for taught just as well as anyone else, sometimes even better.

This brings to mind another revolution—the entrance into the elementary school of an amazing number of men. Where a generation ago all Pleasant Avenue teachers were women, now roughly half are men.

Again, our teachers pronounced this revolution a complete success. For all agreed that a child benefits best when taught by members of both sexes. Some parents lamented that in the past, when boys had been taught by women only, it tended to make some of them weak, passive, and effeminate. But the new method succeeded so well that in our time several parents complained when year after year their children received nothing but women teachers. (Others complained when their children were taught by men only.)

Our teachers saw no correlation between teaching success, sex, and grade taught. That is, they did not believe that women would work out better if they taught just the first, second, and third grades—and men find more success if they concentrated on fourth, fifth and sixth. We had men doing a meritorious job in the second grade. And we had women who taught nothing but sixth grade all their lives—and were good at it.

When I got to this point in my interviews, I found myself thinking more and more often that it is extremely difficult, and maybe even impossible, to describe the good teacher. One day, when a friend asked me, "Who is this good teacher you're always talking about?" I replied, "Why, anyone at all is likely to be a good teacher—anyone at all."

17

One day (I don't recall what the occasion was) it suddenly occurred to me that I, myself, was what our teachers called a good teacher. Yet this was not always so. It happened this way.

I began my teaching career as a high school coach. But I did a poor job there. My teams provided success for other teams. My career provided success for other coaches. Our country was going through the greatest prosperity in its history. Everyone I knew was winning one promotion after another. Yet here I was apparently doing the impossible–working hard, yet failing anyway.

My poor father had starved himself that I might go to college. Among all my relatives I had been the first ever to earn a college diploma. My father had thought that once I got that diploma in my hand I would immediately become a big corporation executive. Everyone who had known me thought that, since I had worked my way through college, I would be more meritorious than other college men and so move from one promotion to another. In reality I couldn't even hold down a job. I was getting fired from town after town.

I wanted to die. I wanted to die. I remember one day thinking. "Why can't I get throat cancer? Thousands die of it. Yet I can't even catch a nose cold."

Then one day a superintendent convinced me to try

elementary school teaching. At first I thought him out of his head. Imagine all those little kids with their running noses and their crying all the time! But I was so desperate I was willing to anything.

I soon learned the old man was right. With his superior mind and his vast experience, he was able to place men in positions where even their own relatives did not dream they belonged. What an advantage it is in life for a young man to run into such a boss.

Almost the minute I moved into grade school physical education my life underwent a revolution. Suddenly everyone around me began referring to me as a good teacher. My principal told salesmen that I was just what he wanted–and at a convention one of them told me. Teachers all acted in a most friendly manner–not conclusive evidence but at least one outward sign of inward quality in a teacher. Even the children fell all over me.

Later one of our teachers told me that he had gone through the same experience, and some others said they had heard of the same thing. They said that many a teacher is good only at one level or grade. Move him from that and his quality seems to vanish. And conversely, many a misfit when moved from the grade he cannot teach, is immediately converted into a good teacher.

18

One of the requirements of this profession is that all practitioners play certain roles. Both professionals and members of the public want to perceive certain qualities in all teachers. Sometimes they do not care if the qualities are really there or not. Just the act will do.

Complying with this, the good teacher sometimes puts on the best act you ever saw in your life. It was probably not for nothing that every morning many of us, on leaving the faculty lounge, said, "Well, I must now go into my act."

The good teacher might even skip nimbly from one role to another. Thus, when in the company of a parent, he might speak something like this: "Listen, we all love this daughter of yours so much, don't be surprised if we try to keep her here forever. I personally am crazy about her."

In the faculty lounge, he might speak this way: "Sandra Keyes is a no good son-of-a-bitch. I predict that three years from now she'll be peddling it on the streets. She's strictly out of the garbage can and on her way to the penitentiary–by way of the relief office. The whole family is like that. I had her older brother a couple of years ago, and he was no damn good either. All cut from the same cloth."

Before the pupil: "Sandra, child, please come here. Is it true what they say–that you wrote a naughty word in your social studies book?"

"All I wrote was, 'Fuck you'."

"NOT SO LOUD. Sandra, I'm not only surprised, but I'm also a little hurt. Now, the girl who wrote those words is not the Sandra I know. Do you want to go through life with people laughing at you? In heaven's name, don't write things like that again—at least not in your own social studies book."

To the principal: "Sandra Keyes! Not again! I thought we had it out about her last week. What is she like? Well, I'll tell you. She sits in the front row with her dress pulled up around her ears. I thought only the girls in high school and college acted that way. She's so young, it's ridiculous. I don't see why I should be saddled with pupils like her year after year."

Throughout the rest of this chapter I am going to list just a few (not all) of the roles Pleasant Avenue teachers said any good teacher should play.

An ancient tradition going back to Socrates and Chaucer pictures the good teacher as wretchedly poor. And to this day people expect teachers to demonstrate conspicuous poverty.

Acting in accordance with this weird expectation, our teachers agreed 100 per cent that the good teacher would try to create an impression of extreme poverty. In that way he would not infuriate the very sensitive taxpayers, some of whom have been known to stand up in public meetings and ask why such-and-such a teacher makes such-and-such a salary.

Some of our teachers entered into a friendly little competition to see who could tell the most gruesome story of poverty. Our principal ($20,000-a-year), for example, drove to work in an old Chevrolet, which he took pains to tell everyone, cost $45. He left his new Oldsmobile 98 at home. This, he explained, was the property of his wife. Incidentally, we thought that the proper car for a shoolteacher was either a second-hand Ford (cheap) or a new Volkswagen (easy on gas).

One of our teachers who was accepted by all the others spoke continually of taking his second-hand Plymouth to the high school auto shop in order to take advantage of the free service. There, the high school boys learned their trade while putting more and more second-hands parts into the thing. However, the last time he had driven in, the shop teacher waved him away. No one could make the thing run any more. Colleague or no colleague, the shop teacher advised him to junk the old klunk. Now what was he supposed to do? How would he get to school?

On top of this, this teacher's wife had just told him that her side was hurting again, and no money in the house for an appendectomy. Well, he was just going to have to send her back to her parents. Actually, they had been supporting his family for years. His brother-in-law, a wealthy electrician, gave him all of his old suits. Look. they almost fitted!

Another teacher told one even better. "I'm a loser," was his favorite and perpetual expression. One day, the faculty met in the cafeteria after school to discuss where to hold the annual Christmas party.

"How about Jake's Bar?" someone asked.

"Oh, heavens no. Not that place," someone else replied. "Prostitutes hang out there."

"I think I can get us Manorhaven Country Club some night in the middle of the week," said this perpetual loser.

"Manorhaven Country Club!" one of the men shouted in amazement. "What would someone like you do in a place like that?"

"I work there after school."

"At what, let me ask?"

"I'm their shoe-shine boy, and a good one, too."

He went on to explain how the club members, if they liked his work, would tip him 25 and 50 cents at a time. "Oh, thank you, sir. God will bless you," he often said to a player, as he crawled around the floor looking for a quarter one had tossed to him. No one tried to beat this true story.

Strangely our teachers did not require that you actually be poor. They only expected that you appear poor. Indeed, some of our wealthiest teachers were also the most respected and beloved. For these complained about their poverty right along with the rest of us.

One was so good at complaining about our low salaries that we elected her to the salary committee. No one argued with the school board members more fiercely than she. She was absolutely fearless. Board members ended up admiring her too.

One year, she stood in front of the faculty and urged all teachers to sign resignations. These she said, she would place in a huge pile in front of the board members at their next meeting and say, "Raise or else!" We experienced teachers began to go crazy from fear. Suppose the board accepted some of the resignations! Not all! Just one here and there! Imagine at 50 being out on the street looking for work! And at a beginner's salary, too! But we did as she suggested. And we won a huge increase.

The next role expected of the good teacher, our teachers said, is that he be conservatively-dressed. For that mythological character is not only good deep down inside, he also looks good. Each morning he presents himself at school freshly bathed, cleanly shaven, and dressed neatly, inexpensively and unostentatiously. Again the intent is not to attract public attention and so possibly criticism.

Correct dress in our time was a dark blue suit, white shirt, and a tie with no design, preferable a black one. White handerkerchief in the lapel pocket would be out, of course. For that would signalize the presence of a person who had the time while dressing to arrange such a thing. Into the lapel instead went thirteen ball-point pens, signalizing that the wearer was a non-nonsense and hard-worker type, a close relative to a shoe clerk–and, therefore, not likely to rouse the envy of any taxpayer. Anything that smacked of wealth, such as French cuffs would, of course, be completely out of the question. No hat, naturally, for this too symbolized the presence of a member of the wealthy class, the members of which had enough money to buy such useless decorations.

Correct facial expression would be dog-face–that of a tired and worn drudge who has for years worked harder than his flesh could bear. A face the color of oatmeal actually conferred esteem; for it told of someone who had no spare time in which to get a suntan. Eyes like fried eggs were also appropriate; they told of someone who had sat up half of the night correcting papers, instead of relaxing or having fun.

Moustaches were out of the question; for they too signalized membership in the rich or leisure class, the members of which have plenty of time in which to trim such things. The sheepherder's haircut (clippers straight up the sides) meant that the wearer was someone interested in getting the most for his money.

Another role expected of any good teacher, our teachers said, is the one in which he demonstrates his loyalty to other teachers. In any school there are usually two sets of laws. First there is the formal one coming from the administrators in the form of orders. This one always says that all teachers would work as hard as possible.

But, contradicting this, there is often an informal rule made by teachers themselves. It says that all teachers should keep the work out-put at a reasonable level. That way all will be able to keep up and no one will look bad. Older teachers tell new ones that we absolutely do not compete with each other. They explain carefully that the burdens are heavy enough around here without anyone proving he could carry even heavier ones.

At Pleasant Avenue this unwritten law produced an atmosphere in which it was most pleasant to work. No one ever competed with anyone else, and the result was much good feeling and harmony.

"You want to know what I did all morning?" a more-or-less typical teacher asked one morning in the faculty lounge. "Nothing. I plan to do the same this afternoon."

"Did you see those students milling around in the hall like a mob?" asked the teacher who sat across from him. "Well, that's my class. Let them kill themselves. I don't care."

But you were only expected to appear lazy. As long as you did it quietly, you could do all the work you liked. Therefore, the best of workers on our faculty often talked as if they were absolutely worthless. One talked in the following manner: "Is the principal in his office today? Because if he isn't, I have a little personal work I want to get done." Then he walked back to his classroom and worked hell out of himself and his kids. He later became a superintendent in another district. No doubt he is a good one.

This obligation to be non-competitive presents a special problem to those teachers who want and deserve promotion. Some solved this by demonstrating not that they were better teachers, but by demonstrating that they were conspicuously lazy. One talked endlessly of how much he regretted that teachers had to work so hard. He spent more time loafing in the faculty lounge than any of the rest of us. By so doing, he let the teachers know that, if he were ever promoted, he would be an easy taskmaster. If, however, he were to speak of grandiose plans for improving the school–which would probably include working the teachers harder–then plenty of them would sabotage and otherwise obstruct his progress.

As you can see by this time, it is no easy task to be a good teacher. Indeed, someone once said that the qualifications for being a good teacher are exactly the same as those for having a good heart attack. Unfortunately, this quip happens to be, oh, so painfully true.

19

Promotion time is always one when teaching quality shows. So many teachers work so hard to get ahead. (One year I asked all our teachers what were their plans for the future. Every man except one said he hoped eventually to become a principal.) Every teacher knows who are the leading candidates, and all discuss the merits of each.

During the time of this study only one Pleasant Avenue teacher won a principalship. All our people agreed that he surely deserved the title of a good teacher. Why? To begin with Warren Able kept such good order in his classrom that even the most hypercritical old lady on our faculty could not find fault.

To demonstrate his conspicuous competency and so perhaps head off criticism, he did things no other teacher could or wanted to. For example, he took off other teachers' hands some of their problem cases. I remember one boy had the habit, if he did not like the teacher's lecture, of pulling his sweater over his head and sinking down below the desk, which of course set the other pupils to laughing. He was, he explained, a human submarine, and was now submerging.

This boy's teacher had taken him to the office, saying his continual antics were driving her crazy. The principal was happy to assign him to Warren's class. There, somehow or other (I don't know how) Warren was able to change the boy into a perfect little gentleman.

I don't think Jack would have dared to have sponsored Warren's career if he had been an incompetent whose only talent was being loyal to Jack. Principals were judged at least partly on their ability to spot talent. We knew one who had his reputation severely damaged when he worked for the promotion of a man who later turned out to be a clinker. Besides, there was so much bitterness at promotion time anyway that if Jack had recommended anyone except a saint and a genius, it would have caused our school to blow up.

During the time of this study two men in other schools in the system were demoted. One, who had been head of the high school English Department, was demoted to just plain teacher again. This cost him $500-a-year. The new superintendent, an old political enemy, simple abolished the position. This, by the way, was a fairly common way for administrators to get rid of enemies who happened to be on tenure. The other unfortunate was an assistant superintendent who got demoted into an elementary school principalship paying a mere $19,000-a-year.

Yet, this experience did not cause other teachers to think less of them. In fact, many the $6,000-a-year teacher who mourned about the poor assistant superintendent. "Fortunes of war," one veteran teacher said. "It is impossible for a teacher to get from one end of his career to the other, without picking up a few such scars."

Even those fired did not lose any esteem. One year, two men came to Pleasant Avenue School from a district to the north of us. Both made no secret of the fact that they had been fired there. Yet both were made to feel most welcome.

Why did we not look down on them? Well, one reason could have been the teachers' traditional sympathy for all underdogs. Because we considered ourselves underdogs. Another reason? All the teachers I ever heard mention the subject said that they had seen it happen again and again that a teacher who failed in one district succeeded in another. Different principals, different pupils, and other circumstances make different demands. Sometimes, the very qualities that make a man a failure in one district, made him a success in another.

For example, one very hard-boiled man, who did not work out in a rich district near us, turned out to be just what we wanted in Pleasant Valley. He fitted in perfectly. Our parents expected the teachers to beat the hell out of the kids. That was the way they treated them at home.

In fact, if you had been fired from some districts, that might cause our teachers to think more of you. This alone might prove that you had courage and principles. "We love trouble-makers," a teachers' association official once said.

Incidentally, all the people who were discharged from our district had no trouble finding excellent positions elsewhere. "Every time I lost a teaching job," said one woman, "I immediately found another one even better." It was good to be a teacher in such times.

In addition to moves up and down the staff ladder, some people make horizontal moves from one district to another. Speaking very generally, our teachers believed that the fewer moves you make, the more respectable you are. If a teacher stays a long time in one place, then the presumption is that he is a success there–that the principal, the other teachers, and the children all like him and make life pleasant for him.

Speaking very generally again, we said more than three moves in a teacher's background does not speak very well for him. Teachers who move every year or two were called by the uncomplimentary term, suitcase teacher.

How much time a teacher spends in any one district also gives a hint about his quality. For the law in most states says that if a teacher works for three years in one district, then this district must rehire him every year thereafter. Naturally, during those three years the principal observes his ability very closely. For he does not want to get stuck with an incompetent. This being the case, if our teachers noticed that someone had lasted only a year or two in several different districts, they inferred he must be a person of very low grade.

The quality of the district from which you moved also could affect your reputation. For some people move from second-rate districts to first-rate ones. Others move in the opposite direction–down. Still others, like second-rate circuses that play only the small towns, move only from one second-rate district to another.

The age of the teacher who moves had an effect on his reputation too. For a young lady or young man to move every year or two would only cause our teachers to laugh. "Still sowing wild oats," they would say. In fact, one man said he would question the drive of any young man who taught in the town where he was born–unless he were born in Beverly Hills, of course. Another said that it would be almost an impossibility for any teacher just out of college to immediately find exactly the right school for him.

After two or three moves, however, one had better have found a place to roost. A man or woman of 40 or 50 still bouncing around was definitely unwelcome. Such people, our teachers suspected, had bad luck clinging to them. And this, we know, can be contagious.

When one of the new schools that I mentioned before opened, this meant not only a promotion for one teacher but also a move for others. Naturally Pleasant Avenue and all the other schools would have to donate some experienced teachers. For you cannot have a new school staffed entirely by teachers right out of college, can you?

But this presented us with a threatening situation. Since we all loved Pleasant Avenue, most of us did not want to move. Every day, therefore, teachers asked each other, "Has Jack picked you to stay? Good I always thought he valued you."

As the names of the teachers who would go, and those who would remain, leaked out, we learned that some teachers were in great demand by both principals–and others were not. The two principals had entered into a friendly little game to see who would get the good teachers–and who would get stuck with the clinkers.

For example, the new principal asked the superintendent to send over our Miss Smith, a crack sixth grade teacher. Two hundred pounds of paranoia! Terrific on discipline! The superintendent agreed, for he wanted a few good teachers in each building. He would not want all the producers in one building, and all the duds in another, would he?

When Jack heard this, he nearly went crazy. "Have you any idea how scarce *good* sixth grade teachers are?" he shouted. "A school is lucky if it has just one. When that one goes, it may take five years to find another. Why is the superintendent taking all my *best* teachers? Is the old man trying to undermine me? No, by God! I absolutely will not part with Miss Smith."

"However," Jack added, "I want to be reasonable. I have in mind the name of another sixth grade teacher I'll be glad to send along. Mr. Blanc."

"Blanc!" exclaimed the new principal. "No thanks." Apparently, someone had already talked to him about the quality of our different teachers.

After much arguing and some hard feeling, finally the division of the faculty was made. As we surveyed the wreckage, we said that surely to God our principal would not dare to ship out all the incompetents and keep all the good teachers for himself.

But he did.

20

One year quickly followed another. I think the time flew because I was enjoying my work so much. In fact, looking back on it all now, I believe I was living through some of the best years of my life.

Years ago, as a serviceman, I used to press my face against the window of the troop train as it raced through the little towns. I wanted to see the public school in each. There it was. Like a medieval cathedral, it was always the largest, the most expensive, and the most beautiful building in town. Now I worked in just such a building. Not a bad place to spend your life, if you ask me.

As the years passed I began to grow a few grey hairs. I wondered what effect all of this experience and age would have on my reputation in Pleasant Avenue School. I decided to ask some questions. I heard some very interesting answers.

You might think that the experienced teachers would all enjoy excellent reputations, and the new ones would belong to a kind of lower order. But again it was not this way at all. In fact, experienced teachers would be delighted to point out that some of the most respected people had been in the profession only a few months. Then they would tell you that some of the most hopeless bunglers had been around for years and years–and were still bungling.

Our teachers believed that a teacher sells a perishable product–himself. The longer he teaches, the less efficient he becomes. He loses a little along the way. Each year sees a loss. True, at first there is a period of four or five years, when the teacher is straight out of college, when he profits by experience. After that, he either stays the same–or he goes into a slow decline.

The newer teachers, thinking that they had to work very hard to keep up with the veterans, really gave all. They sponsored student clubs, took university courses, visited the homes of the youngsters (to know them better), and worked long after closing time–little realizing that the veteran teacher never does any of these things any more.

"I'm teaching my third graders French," said one young lady who might have looked just fine on the cover of a movie magazine. She did not have to teach French. She did it because she wanted to.

"We're going to put out a class newspaper," said one young man, who looked as though he were a minor executive in some bank. Soon his pupils were going from door to door asking questions. Naturally, he had to do all the typing and mimeographing, but he did not mind this extra work. In fact, he enjoyed it.

"Say, are those bus windows supposed to be up or down?" another young man asked. He had just reprimanded some pupils for putting their hands out the windows.

"I really don't know," an experienced teacher replied somwhat annoyed. "Now wasn't that just like a new teacher to ask a dumb question like that?" he later asked me. "An experienced teacher would not care what the children did with their dear little hands."

However, with time all these beautiful young people lost their drive, their interest, and their teaching efficiency. Maybe it was the large classes that sapped their energy, until by January they could do nothing but teach out of a textbook. Maybe it was the boredom, the continual disappointment, the routine, the cheap politics, the lack of recognition, or the constant repression from above. Maybe it was the poor example we older teachers set. Who knows? Whatever the reason, all of these enthusiastic and energetic young people slowly became tired and worn, dispirited and disillusioned, crafty and corrupt just like the rest of us.

Well, if we saw no beneficial connection between experience and teaching efficiency, then how come we teachers respected the experienced so much? I think the reason might have been our belief that mere survival in this profession is no small accomplishment. Turnover in all public schools in this country runs about ten per cent per year. Anyone who lasts long enough to get on tenure or until retirement is no run-of-the-mill person. He is made of steel.

The students eliminate many. Superintendents, going crazy trying to find enough teachers, may hire anyone they can get their hands on, just to make up a complete faculty. But the pupils, being absolutely incorruptible, would not allow anyone to stick around who does not have genuine teaching quality. They put every newcomer through a process of elimination that will eliminate all but the most excellent.

For example, several high-spirited sixth grade boys, once emptied their squirt guns full of black ink down the front of one man's white suit. He was standing there explaining to the bored class the difference between regular and irregular verbs. And they sat there laughing and firing away. They knew they had nothing to fear from this mild-mannered, infinitely refined, and unfailingly polite young man.

When the principal heard about this, all he said was: "Say, they didn't get any of that ink on the floor, did they? It's hell to get off, you know."

The administrators eliminate others. To be sure, we had some genuine princes for superintendents and principals. But we had some mediocrities too. There was a brief ceremony the night one old lady retired. After listening to speeches eulogizing her, this grand old lady accepted the traditional dozen roses on the stage, then drove home with us. Though she had kept pretty quiet until then, on the ride home she remarked on what a bastard the superintendent had been. For years, she said, he had been trying to get rid of her. He did not like experienced teachers. They made too much money.

He preferred beginning teachers, who made only minimum salaries.

She added that over the years she had picked up a few enemies among the teachers too. And these did not make her stay any more pleasant. One day, for example, she had let slip the remark that she knew some teachers who were incompetent. Hearing this, one teacher screamed that she must mean him–because the description fit him exactly. Everyone in the school district would automatically know whom she meant. He was insulted. Every teacher picked up a few of these, she said–if he lasted long enough.

Another interesting way our teachers judged teachers goes this way. Some teachers saw great meaning in the date a teacher started at Pleasant Avenue. For example, if you said you came during the superintendency of Mr. Worth, that suggested that you had real quality. For Mr. Worth went to great pains with his recruiting. He would fly to Boston or New York, just to see one good candidate.

He also knew how the get rid of the dead wood–by making life miserable for them. So, if you left the system during the tenure of Mr. Worth, that suggested something about your quality, too.

However, if you arrived during the time when Mr. Lacy was the superintendent, that did not speak too well for you. For Lacy had little interest in recruiting. When he needed new teachers, he simply picked up the telephone and asked a nearby placement agency to send over a batch–so many sixth grade teachers, so many high school English teachers, then he hung up the phone, and that was that.

In the last chapter I mentioned the tenure law which in almost all states says that any teacher who has worked for three years in a district cannot be discharged–unless he becomes insubordinate, immoral, or grossly incompetent. The intent of this law is to give teachers some very badly needed job security. In this connection it is interesting to ask, could not so much job security result–in some cases–in boredom, slothfulness, and finally stupidity? For example, what if a teacher worked just hard enough to get on tenure, then took it easy?

Judging from conversations I overheard and from numerous direct questions I asked, I would say that this would be a physical impossibility. For, if any teacher did not do enough work, our principal simply transferred him to a class composed of 100 per cent troublemakers, a class filled with gems each with the reputation of having broken the hearts of every teacher who tried to do anything for him. It did not make much difference whether this teacher taught anything or not. By doing work that no one else wanted, this teacher had value anyway.

Closely related to experience is the very touchy subject of age. Generally speaking, our teachers believed that age has no effect on teaching efficiency. In some other occupations, such as selling, it is true that the practitioner may be all worn out and used as early as 40. But in other occupations, such as medicine, law, and teaching, the practitioner has value right up until the day he falls into the grave. Some who joined our staff in middle age had just as good reputations as those who came to us right out of college. Two ladies in their late 60's were the most respected members of our whole faculty. And this by both teachers and students.

The superintendent and the principal both said they valued these oldsters. Jack said that where many a younger teacher taught only a year or two, then got married or moved away, these older ones came back year after year. He knew he could depend on them, and he was right. He called them the backbone of our faculty.

Indeed, the reader may not realize it, but when he sees some tired, worn, and wrinkled old lady dragging herself up the steps of the school, he often sees at the same time someone whom both administrators and teachers respect very much. She also is a good teacher.

21

One day near the close of my sixth year, the superintendent called me into his office and told me he was transferring me to a new school. I protested. For I had been very happy at Pleasant Avenue. But he was kind enough to describe the move as a kind of quasi-promotion. The gym in the new school would be larger. I would have an assistant—and later on, maybe even more money.

My last day at Pleasant Avenue was memorable. On the last day of school, there was always some closing ceremony. The local postmaster, or some other great dignitary, gave a speech. At this one, the owner of a prominent local filling station talked on the new frontiers awaiting all young people in outer space. The children sang. I wonder if there is anything more beautiful than the sound of children singing. The whole ceremony put you in mind of the times when you stood on a stage very similar to this one and sang the same kind of songs, long, long ago.

Then, for the last time, all the children marched down the hall and out the door. Each of the teachers stood outside his or her classroom and said "good-by" to all who passed. Many of the little girls were crying; for the children also dearly loved this school. A few of the younger women teachers wept too.

On this particular day, one of the little boys, who had been my unofficial assistant, stepped out of line and stood next to me. He said that he had always liked me and that he had learned a lot from me. I thanked him and added rhetorically that I had learned a lot from him and the other people at Pleasant Avenue too. He finally got back into line and we waved good-bye to each other.

Then I went to my office and began to gather up my personal belongings. But as I sat in the quiet, I thought back on the truth of the remark I had made out in the hall. Yes, I had learned a lot at Pleasant Avenue.

I learned, for example, that it is not easy and maybe even impossible to identify a good teacher. I will never again judge a teacher by his title, age, personal appearance, or educational background.

I learned that no teacher is good all the time. Nor is any one good for all students. The best of teachers still cannot reach some students.

I came to believe that there is not just one personality structure which all teachers should have. Since the children themselves differ so much one from another, then perhaps they are taught best by a faculty with all kinds of different personalities on it.

I learned, furthermore, that when a good teacher is present, then any teaching method seems to work. But without a good teacher, no method works. No method and no equipment, however expensive, is any better than the teacher who uses it.

Most important, I learned that the definition of a good teacher sometimes differs from one district to another. Not only rich districts have standards. Poor districts have them too. The requirements in poor districts may be a little different. But they are no less demanding. Indeed, it might be that there is a different definition of the good teacher in every school in the land. Worse, perhaps this definition changes from time to time.

Looking back, I suspect that faculties sometimes manufacture their own good teachers. For they cause some teachers to fail and others to succeed. I feel that this one made a success of me. I will always be grateful.